PRINCIPLES OF FEDERAL APPROPRIATIONS LAW (ANNUAL UPDATE OF THE THIRD EDITION)

PRINCIPLES OF FEDERAL APPROPRIATIONS LAW (ANNUAL UPDATE OF THE THIRD EDITION)

UNITED STATES GOVERNMENT ACCOUNTABILITY OFFICE

Nova Science Publishers, Inc.
New York

For permission to use material from this book please contact us:
Telephone 631-231-7269; Fax 631-231-8175
Web Site: http://www.novapublishers.com

LIBRARY OF CONGRESS CATALOGING-IN-PUBLICATION DATA

Available Upon Request
ISBN: 978-1-60456-972-8

Published by Nova Science Publishers, Inc. ✣ New York

CONTENTS

PREFACE

The authors are pleased to present the annual update of the third edition of Volumes I and II of *Principles of Federal Appropriations Law.* The objective in this publication is to present a cumulative supplement to the published third edition text that includes all relevant decisions from January 1 to December 31, 2007. After Volume III is published, the third edition of *Principles* will be complete and all three volumes will be updated annually.

The annual update is posted electronically on GAO's Web site (www.gao.gov). These annual updates are not issued in hard copy and should be used as electronic supplements. Users should retain hard copies of the third edition volumes and refer to the cumulative updates for newer material. The page numbers identified in the annual update as containing new material are the page numbers in the hard copy of the third edition and the new, updated information appears as bolded text.

VOLUME 1

FORWARD*

Page i – Insert the following as footnote number 1 at the end of the first paragraph (after "GAO Legal Products."[1]):

[1] Section 8 of the GAO Human Capital Reform Act of 2004, Pub. L. No. 108-271, 118 Stat. 811, 814 (July 7, 2004), 31 U.S.C. § 702 note, changed GAO's name to the "Government Accountability Office." This change was made to better reflect GAO's current mission. *See* S. Rep. No. 108-216, at 8 (2003); H.R. Rep. No. 108-380, at 12 (2003). Therefore, any reference in this volume to the "General Accounting Office" should be read to mean "Government Accountability Office." The acronym "GAO" as used in the text now refers to the Government Accountability Office.

---

* Excerpted from GAO Report GAO-08-450SP, dated March 2008.

Chapter 1

INTRODUCTION

B. THE CONGRESSIONAL "POWER OF THE PURSE"

Page 1-4 – Replace footnote 6 with the following:

[6] Numerous similar statements exist. *See, e.g., Knote v. United States,* 95 U.S. 149, 154 (1877); *Marathon Oil Co. v. United States,* 374 F.3d 1123, 1133–34 (Fed. Cir. 2004), *cert. denied,* 544 U.S. 1031 (2005);

Gowland v. Aetna, 143 F.3d 951, 955 (5th Cir. 1998); *Hart's Case,* 16 Ct. Cl. 459, 484 (1880), *aff'd, Hart v. United States,* 118 U.S. 62 (1886);

Jamal v. Travelers Lloyds of Texas Insurance Co., 131 F. Supp. 2d 910, 919 (S.D. Tex. 2001); *Doe v. Mathews,* 420 F. Supp. 865, 870–71 (D. N.J. 1976).

Page 1-5 – Insert the following after the second paragraph:

For example, in *Rumsfeld v. Forum for Academic and Institutional Rights, Inc.,* 547 U.S. 47 (2006), the Supreme Court reversed a lower court decision, 390 F.3d 219 (3rd Cir. 2004), and upheld the constitutionality of the so-called "Solomon Amendment." Originally enacted as an appropriation rider and now codified as amended at 10 U.S.C. § 983, the Solomon Amendment generally prohibits the receipt of certain federal funds by institutions of higher education that deny military recruiters the same access they provide to other recruiters on their campuses. The Forum for Academic and Institutional Rights (FAIR), an association of law schools and faculty members, maintained that the Solomon Amendment attached an unconstitutional condition to their receipt of federal funds and, thus, exceeded congressional constitutional authority under the so-called "Spending Clause" in article I, section 8. Specifically, FAIR alleged that the statute violated their First Amendment rights to oppose federal policies regarding homosexuals in the military. In an 8–0 opinion by Chief Justice Roberts, the Supreme Court rejected these arguments. Quoting from *Grove City College v. Bell,* 465 U.S. 555, 575–76 (1984), the Court noted that under the Spending Clause, "Congress is free to attach reasonable and unambiguous conditions to federal financial assistance that educational institutions are not obliged to accept." 547 U.S. at 59. In essence, the Court reasoned that funding conditions such as the Solomon Amendment cannot violate the Spending Clause if Congress could constitutionally impose the same requirements through direct legislation. The Court went on to hold that Congress could enact legislation that directly mandated the Solomon Amendment's requirements without running afoul of the First Amendment. *Id.* at 59–60. The Court observed that Congress could use its authority under article I, section 8, clauses 1 and 12–13 of the Constitution to provide for the common defense and to raise and support armies,*etc.,* as a basis for directly legislating the Solomon Amendment's requirements for equal access by military recruiters so long as the legislation was otherwise constitutional. It then held that the Solomon Amendment's requirements did not implicate First Amendment rights, dismissing each of FAIR's arguments to the contrary. The opinion stated by way of summary:

> "The Solomon Amendment neither limits what law schools may say nor requires them to say anything. . . . As a general matter, the Solomon Amendment regulates conduct, not speech. It affects what law schools must *do*—afford equal access to military recruiters—not what they may or not *say.*"
>
> *Id.* at 60 (emphasis in original).

Page 1-7 – Insert the following after the last paragraph:

In a 2007 decision, GAO declined to interpret the voluntary services prohibition of the Antideficiency Act to prohibit the President from exercising his constitutional power to make a recess appointment to an individual who was barred by statute from receiving compensation. B-309301, June 8, 2007. GAO noted that "serious constitutional issues would arise if [the statutory bar on compensation], in conjunction with the voluntary services prohibition, were read to directly restrict the President from making a recess appointment." *Id.* at 6.

Page 1-9 – Replace the first paragraph with the following:

In *Kansas v. United States,* 214 F.3d 1196, 1201–02, n.6 (10th Cir.), *cert. denied,* 531 U.S. 1035 (2000), the court noted that there were few decisions striking down federal statutory spending conditions.[9]

However, there are two recent interesting examples of situations in which courts invalidated a spending condition on First Amendment grounds. In *Legal Services Corp. v. Velasquez,* 531 U.S. 533 (2001), a conditional provision (contained in the annual appropriations for the Legal Service Corporation (LSC) since 1996) was struck down as inconsistent with the First Amendment. This provision prohibited LSC grantees from representing clients in efforts to amend or otherwise challenge existing welfare law. The Supreme Court found this provision interfered with the free speech rights of clients represented by LSC-funded attorneys.[10] In *American Civil Liberties Union (ACLU) v. Mineta,* 319 F. Supp. 2d 69 (D.D.C. 2004), the court declared unconstitutional an appropriation provision forbidding the use of federal mass transit grant funds for any activity that promoted the legalization or medical use of marijuana, for example, posting an advertisement on a bus. Relying on *Legal Services Corp.,* the court held that the provision constituted "viewpoint discrimination" in violation of the First Amendment. *ACLU,* 319 F. Supp. 2d at 83–87.

Page 1-10 – Insert the following after the first partial paragraph:

There have been some recent court cases upholding congressional actions attaching conditions to the use of federal funds that require states to waive their sovereign immunity from lawsuits under the Eleventh Amendment. In these cases, courts found the condition a legitimate exercise of Congress's spending power. For example, the court in *Barbour v. Washington Metropolitan Transit Authority,* 374 F.3d 1161 (D.C. Cir. 2004), *cert. denied,* 544 U.S. 904 (2005), upheld a statutory provision known as the "Civil Rights Remedies Equalization Act," 42 U.S.C. § 2000d-7, which clearly conditioned a state's acceptance of federal funds on its waiver of its Eleventh Amendment immunity to suits under various federal antidiscrimination laws. Among other things, the court rejected an argument based on *Dole* that the condition was not sufficiently related to federal spending. The opinion observed that the Supreme Court has never overturned Spending Clause legislation on "relatedness grounds." *Barbour,* 374 F.3d at 1168.

Similarly, two courts rejected challenges to section 3 of the Religious Land Use and Institutionalized Persons Act of 2000 (RLUIPA), 42 U.S.C. § 2000cc-1, which limits restrictions on the exercise of religion by persons institutionalized in a program or activity that receives federal financial assistance. *Charles v. Verhagen,* 348 F.3d 601 (7th Cir. 2003); *Williams v. Bitner,* 285 F. Supp. 2d 593 (M.D. Pa. 2003), *aff'd in part, remanded in part* 455 F.3d 186 (3rd Cir. 2006). In *Charles,* the court held that RLUIPA "falls squarely within Congress' pursuit of the general welfare under its Spending

Clause authority." *Charles,* 348 F.3d at 607. The court also rejected the argument that the statute's restrictions could not be related to a federal spending interest because the state corrections program at issue received less than 2 percent of its budget from federal funding: "Nothing within Spending Clause jurisprudence, or RLUIPA for that matter, suggests that States are bound by the conditional grant of federal money only if the State receives or derives a certain percentage . . . of its budget from federal funds." *Id.* at 609.

Page 1-10 – Replace the second paragraph with the following:

For some additional recent cases upholding statutory funding conditions, see *Biodiversity Associates v. Cables,* 357 F.3d 1152 (10th Cir.), *cert. denied,* 543 U.S. 817 (2004) (upholding an appropriations rider that explicitly superseded a settlement agreement the plaintiffs had reached with the Forest Service in environmental litigation); *Kansas v. United States,* 214 F.3d 1196 (10th Cir.), *cert. denied,* 531 U.S. 1035 (2000) (upholding the statutory requirement conditioning receipt of federal block grants used to provide cash assistance and other supportive services to low income families on a state's participation in and compliance with a federal child support enforcement program); *Litman,* 186 F.3d 544 (state university's receipt of federal funds was validly conditioned upon waiver of the state's Eleventh Amendment immunity from federal antidiscrimination lawsuits); *California v. United States,* 104 F.3d 1086, 1092 (9th Cir. 1997) (acknowledging that although it originally agreed to the condition for receipt of federal Medicaid funds on state provision of emergency medical services to illegal aliens, California now viewed that condition as coerced because substantial increases in illegal immigration left California with no choice but to remain in the program to prevent collapse of its medical system; the complaint was dismissed for failure to state a claim upon which relief could be granted); and *Armstrong v. Vance,* 328 F. Supp. 2d 50 (D.D.C. 2004) and *Whatley v. District of Columbia,* 328 F. Supp. 2d 15 (D.D.C. 2004), *aff'd,* 447 F.3d 814 (D.C. Cir. 2006) (two related decisions upholding appropriations provisions that imposed a cap on the District of Columbia's payment of attorney fees awarded in litigation under the Individuals with Disabilities Education Act, 20 U.S.C. § § 1400–1490). See also Richard W. Garnett, *The New Federalism, the Spending Power, and Federal Criminal Law,* 89 Cornell L.

Rev. 1 (Nov. 2003), an article that provides more background on this general subject.

Page 1-12 – Replace the second bullet in the first paragraph with the following:

- Agencies may not spend, or commit themselves to spend, in advance of or in excess of appropriations. 31 U.S.C. § 1341 (Antideficiency Act). GAO has said that because the Antideficiency Act is central to Congress's core constitutional power of the purse, GAO will not interpret general language in another statute, such as the "notwithstanding any other provision of law" clause, to imply a waiver of the Act without some affirmative expression of congressional intent to give the agency the authority to obligate in advance or in excess of an appropriation. B-303961, Dec. 6, 2004.

D. "LIFE CYCLE" OF AN APPROPRIATION

3. Budget Execution and Control

Page 1-34 – Insert the following after the first partial paragraph:

In 2006, GAO reported to Congress that in 13 instances executive agencies had impounded funds that the President had proposed for cancellation. B-308011, Aug. 4, 2006; B-307122.2, Mar. 2, 2006. When the President proposed cancellation of these funds, the Administration had not submitted reports of impoundments under the Impoundment Control Act because, officials explained, the Administration was not withholding funds from obligation. In all 13 instances, the agencies released impounded funds as a result of GAO's inquiries. *Id.*

E. THE ROLE OF THE ACCOUNTING OFFICERS: LEGAL DECISIONS

2. Decisions of the Comptroller General

Page 1-40 – Replace the last partial paragraph with the following:

There is no specific procedure for requesting a decision from the Comptroller General. A simple letter is usually sufficient. The request should, however, include all pertinent information or supporting material and should present any arguments the requestor wishes to have considered. *See* GAO, *Procedures and Practices for Legal Decisions and Opinions,* GAO-06-1064SP (Washington, D.C.: Sept. 2006), *available at* www.gao.gov/legal/ resources.html.

Page 1-42 – Replace the third full paragraph with the following:

For example, as we discussed earlier in this chapter, effective June 30, 1996, Congress transferred claims settlement authority under 31 U.S.C. § 3302 to the Director of the Office of Management and Budget (OMB). Congress gave the director of OMB the authority to delegate this function to such agency or agencies as he deemed appropriate. *See, e.g.,* B-302996, May 21, 2004 (GAO no longer has authority to settle a claim for severance pay); B-278805, July 21, 1999 (the International Trade Commission was the appropriate agency to resolve the subject claims request).

Page 1-42 – Replace the fourth full paragraph with the following:

Other areas where the Comptroller General will decline to render decisions include questions concerning which the determination of another agency is by law "final and conclusive." Examples are determinations on the merits of a claim against another agency under the Federal Tort Claims Act (28 U.S.C. § 2672) or the Military Personnel and Civilian Employees' Claims Act of 1964 (31 U.S.C. § 3721). *See, e.g.,* B-300829, Apr. 4, 2004 (regarding the Military Personnel and Civilian Employees' Claims Act). Another example is a decision by the Secretary of Veterans Affairs on a claim for veterans' benefits (38 U.S.C. § 511). *See* B-266193, Feb. 23, 1996; 56 Comp. Gen. 587, 591 (1977); B-226599.2, Nov. 3, 1988 (nondecision letter).

3. Other Relevant Authorities

Page 1-48 – Replace paragraph number 7 with the following:

7. A Glossary of Terms Used in the Federal Budget Process, GAO-05-734SP (Washington, D.C.: Sept. 2005)—This publication contains standard definitions of fiscal and budgetary terms. It is published by GAO as required by 31 U.S.C. § 1112(c), and is updated periodically.

Chapter 2

THE LEGAL FRAMEWORK

B. SOME BASIC CONCEPTS

1. What Constitutes an Appropriation

Page 2-20 – Insert the following after the second full paragraph:

Subsequent to the *Core Concepts* and *AINS* decisions, the Third Circuit Court of Appeals had occasion to weigh in on the issue of revolving funds in a non-Tucker Act situation in *American Federation of Government Employees (AFGE) v. Federal Labor Relations Authority (FLRA)*, 388 F.3d 405 (3rd Cir. 2004). In that case, AFGE, representing Army depot employees, had proposed an amendment to the employees' collective bargaining agreement that would have required the Army to pay reimbursements of personal expenses incurred by the depot employees as a result of cancelled annual leave from a defense working capital fund. When the Army objected that it had no authority to use the working capital fund for personal expenses, AFGE appealed to FLRA. FLRA agreed with the Army and ruled that the provision was "nonnegotiable." Citing FLRA decisions, Comptroller General decisions, and federal court cases, FLRA concluded that the working capital fund, a revolving fund, is treated as a continuing appropriation and, as such, the fund was not available for reimbursement of personal expenses.

The court agreed with FLRA that the defense working capital fund consists of appropriated funds and is thus not available to pay the personal expenses of Army employees. The court, however, rejected what it called "FLRA's blanket generalization that revolving funds are always appropriations." *AFGE,* 388 F.3d at 411. Instead, the court applied a standard used by the Federal Circuit and the Court of Federal Claims when addressing the threshold issue of Tucker Act jurisdiction, a "clear expression" standard; that is, funds should be regarded as "appropriated" absent a "clear expression by Congress that the agency was to be separated from the general federal revenues." *Id.* at 410. The court observed in this regard:

> "While that 'clear expression' standard arises in the context of Tucker Act jurisprudence, we think it accurately reflects the broader principle that one should not lightly presume that Congress meant to surrender its control over public expenditures by authorizing an entity to be entirely self-sufficient and outside the appropriations process. . . . For this reason, the courts have sensibly treated agency money as appropriated even when the agency is fully financed by outside revenues, so long as Congress has not clearly stated that it wishes to relinquish the control normally afforded through the appropriations process.
>
> * * * * * * * * * *
>
> " . . . [W]e think the correct rule is that the characterization of a government fund as appropriated or not depends entirely on Congress' expression, whatever the actual source of the money and whether or not the fund operates on a revolving rather than annualized basis."

Id. at 410–11. In applying this standard to the particular funding arrangement at issue, the court determined that the defense working capital fund was not a nonappropriated fund instrumentality and upheld the FLRA decision. "What matters is how Congress wishes to treat government revenues, not the source of the revenues." Id. at 413.

3. Transfer and Reprogramming

Page 2-24 – Replace footnote 40 with the following:

[40] 7 Comp. Gen. 524 (1928); 4 Comp. Gen. 848 (1925); 17 Comp. Dec. 174 (1910). Cases in which adequate statutory authority was found to exist are B-302760, May 17, 2004 (the transfer of funds from the Library of Congress to the Architect of the Capitol for construction of a loading dock at the Library is authorized) and B-217093, Jan. 9, 1985 (the transfer from the Japan-United States Friendship Commission to the Department of Education to partially fund a study of Japanese education is authorized).

Page 2-25 – Insert the following after the first full paragraph:

In 2007, GAO found that the Department of Homeland Security's (DHS) Preparedness Directorate had authority pursuant to 31 U.S.C. § 1534, the "account adjustment statute," to fund shared services that benefited the directorate as a whole by initially obligating the services against one appropriation within the directorate and then allocating the costs to the benefiting appropriations. However, the Directorate did not appear to properly allocate the costs. To the extent it did not properly record its obligations prior to the end of the fiscal year against each benefiting appropriation for the estimated value of the services each appropriation received, as required by the account adjustment statute, the Directorate improperly augmented its appropriations. B-308762, Sept. 17, 2007.

Page 2-28 – Insert the following, including the reference to new footnote number 44a, after the first full paragraph:

In another case, GAO found that the Department of Defense (DOD) improperly "parked" DOD funds when it transferred the funds to a Department of the Interior franchise fund, GovWorks.[44a] B-308944, July 17, 2007. "Parking" is a term used to describe a transfer of appropriations to a revolving fund to extend the availability of the appropriations. GovWorks is a revolving fund established to provide common administrative services to Interior and other agencies by procuring goods and services from vendors on behalf of federal agencies on a competitive basis. DOD used Military Interdepartmental Purchase Requests (MIPRs) to transfer funds to GovWorks but did not identify the specific items or services that DOD wanted GovWorks to acquire on its behalf until after the funds had expired. DOD subsequently improperly directed GovWorks to use expired DOD funds for contracts in violation of the *bona fide* needs rule.

Page 2-28 – Insert the following as new footnote number 44a:

[44a] GovWorks is officially known as the Acquisition Services Directorate. *See* www.govworks.gov (last visited Feb. 8, 2008).

Page 2-31 – Replace the first full paragraph with the following and insert new footnote number 48a as follows:

Thus, as a matter of law, an agency is free to reprogram unobligated funds as long as the expenditures are within the general purpose of the appropriation and are not in violation of any other specific limitation or otherwise prohibited. *E.g.*, B-279338, Jan. 4, 1999; B-123469, May 9, 1955. This is true even though the agency may already have administratively allotted the funds to a particular object. 20 Comp. Gen. 631 (1941). In some situations, an agency may be required to reprogram funds to satisfy other obligations. *E.g., Cherokee Nation of Oklahoma v. Leavitt,* 543 U.S. 631, 641–43 (2005) (government must reprogram unrestricted funds to cover contractual obligations);[48a] *Blackhawk Heating and Plumbing,* 622 F.2d at 552 n.9 (satisfaction of obligations under a settlement agreement).

Page 2-31 – Insert the following for new footnote number 48a:

[48a] In this case, the government had argued that its contracts with Indian tribes were not "ordinary procurement contracts," so it was not legally bound to pay certain contract costs unless Congress appropriated sufficient funds for that purpose. The Court found the tribal contracts to be binding in the same way as ordinary contractual promises and that the government would have to reprogram appropriations to fulfill its contractual obligations to the tribes, notwithstanding that the government may have planned to use those appropriations for other purposes that the government felt were critically important.

4. General Provisions: When Construed as Permanent Legislation

Page 2-36 – Replace the third full paragraph with the following:

The words "this or any other act" may be used in conjunction with other language that makes the result, one way or the other, indisputable. The provision is clearly not permanent if the phrase "during the current fiscal year" is added. *Norcross v. United States,* 142 Ct. Cl. 763 (1958). Addition of the phrase "with respect to any fiscal year" would indicate, all other potential considerations aside, that Congress intended the provision to be permanent. B-230110, *supra.* For example, in the 2006 Department of Justice Appropriations Act, as part of the language of ATF's Salaries and Expenses appropriation, Congress included a proviso stating that "no funds appropriated under this or any other Act with respect to any fiscal year may be used to disclose part or all of the contents of the Firearms Trace System database" to anyone other than a law enforcement agency or a prosecutor in connection with a criminal investigation or prosecution. Pub. L., No. 109-108, title I, 119 Stat. 2290, 2295 (Nov. 22, 2005). In B-309704, Aug. 28, 2007, GAO determined that the proviso constituted permanent legislation because the forward-looking effect of the phrase "this or any other Act" coupled with the phrase "with respect to any fiscal year" indicates Congress's intention that the provision be permanent.

C. Relationship of Appropriations to Other Types of Legislation

2. Specific Problem Areas and the Resolution of Conflicts

Page 2-43 – Replace the third full paragraph with the following:

Second, Congress is free to amend or repeal prior legislation as long as it does so directly and explicitly and does not violate the Constitution. It is also possible for one statute to implicitly amend or repeal a prior statute, but it is firmly established that "repeal by implication" is disfavored, and statutes will be construed to avoid this result whenever reasonably possible. *E.g.*, *Tennessee Valley Authority v. Hill,* 437 U.S. 153, 189–90 (1978); *Morton v. Mancari,* 417 U.S. 535, 549 (1974); *Posadas v. National City Bank of New York,* 296 U.S. 497, 503 (1936); B-307720, Sept. 27, 2007; B-290011, Mar. 25, 2002; B-261589, Mar. 6, 1996; 72 Comp. Gen. 295, 297 (1993); 68 Comp. Gen. 19, 22–23 (1988); 64 Comp. Gen. 143, 145 (1984); 58 Comp. Gen. 687, 691–92 (1979); B-258163, Sept. 29, 1994; B-236057, May 9, 1990. Repeals by implication are particularly disfavored in the appropriations context. *Robertson v. Seattle Audubon Society,* 503 U.S. 429, 440 (1992).

Page 2-44 – Replace the first full paragraph with the following:

A corollary to the "cardinal rule" against repeal by implication, or perhaps another way of saying the same thing, is the rule of construction that statutes should be construed harmoniously so as to give maximum effect to both wherever possible. *E.g., Posadas,* 296 U.S. at 503; *Strawser v. Atkins,* 290 F.3d 720 (4th Cir.), *cert. denied,* 537 U.S. 1045 (2002); B-290011, Mar. 25, 2002; 53 Comp. Gen. 853, 856 (1974); B-208593.6, Dec. 22, 1988. See B-307720, Sept. 27, 2007, and B-258000, Aug. 31, 1994, for examples of harmonizing ambiguous appropriation and authorization provisions in order to effectuate congressional intent.

Page 2-44 – Replace the second full paragraph with the following:

Third, if two statutes are in irreconcilable conflict, the more recent statute, as the latest expression of Congress, governs. As one court concluded in a statement illustrating the eloquence of simplicity, "[t]he statutes are thus in conflict, the earlier permitting and the later prohibiting," so the later statute supersedes the earlier. *Eisenberg v. Corning,* 179 F.2d 275, 277 (D.C. Cir. 1949). In a sense, the "last in time" rule is yet another way of expressing the repeal by implication principle. We state it separately to highlight its narrowness: it applies only when the two statutes cannot be reconciled in any reasonable manner, and then only to the extent of the conflict. *E.g.,*

B-308715, Apr. 20, 2007 ("It is well established that a later enacted, specific statute will typically supersede a conflicting previously enacted, general statute to the extent of the inconsistency."). *See also Posadas,* 296 U.S. at 503; B-255979, Oct. 30, 1995; B-226389, Nov. 14, 1988; B-214172, July 10, 1984, *aff'd upon reconsideration,* 64 Comp. Gen. 282 (1985).

Page 2-69 – Insert the following new paragraphs, including the reference to new footnote number 60a, after the first full paragraph:

Recently, two courts have interpreted appropriation restrictions to avoid repeal by implication: *City of Chicago v. Department of the Treasury,* 384 F.3d 429 (7th Cir. 2004), and *City of New York v. Beretta U.S.A. Corp.,* 222 F.R.D. 51 (E.D. N.Y. 2004). In the first case, the City of Chicago had sued the former Bureau of Alcohol, Tobacco, and Firearms under the Freedom of Information Act (FOIA), 5 U.S.C. § 552, to obtain access to certain information from the agency's firearms databases. The Court of Appeals for the Seventh Circuit held that the information was not exempt from disclosure under FOIA. *City of Chicago v. Department of the Treasury,* 287 F.3d 628 (7th Cir. 2002). The agency then appealed to the Supreme Court. While the appeal was pending, Congress enacted appropriations language for fiscal years 2003 and 2004 providing that no funds shall be available or used to take any action under FOIA or otherwise that would publicly disclose the information. Pub. L. No. 108-7, div. J, title VI, § 644, 117 Stat. 11, 473 (Feb. 20, 2003); Pub. L. No. 108-199, div. B, title I, 118 Stat. 3, 53 (Jan. 23, 2004). The Supreme Court remanded the case to the Seventh Circuit to consider the impact, if any, of the appropriations language. *Department of Justice v. City of Chicago,* 537 U.S. 1229 (2003). In *City of Chicago v. Department of the Treasury,* 384 F.3d 429 (7th Cir. 2004), the court decided that the appropriations language had essentially no impact on the case. Citing a number of cases on the rule disfavoring implied repeals (particularly by appropriations act), the court held that the appropriations rider did not repeal FOIA or otherwise affect the agency's legal obligation to release the information in question. The court concluded that "FOIA deals only peripherally with the allocation of funds—its main focus is to ensure agency information is made available to the public." *Id.* at 435. In this regard, the court repeatedly emphasized the minimal costs entailed in complying with the access request and concluded that "there is no 'irreconcilable conflict' between prohibiting the use of federal funds to process the request and granting the City access to the databases." *Id.* After the 2004 decision, the agency filed a request for rehearing. Before the rehearing, Congress passed the Consolidated Appropriations Act of 2005 specifying that no funds be used to provide the data sought by the City, and further provided that the data be "immune from judicial process." Pub. L. No. 108-447, div. B, title I, 118 Stat. 2809, 2859 (Dec. 8, 2004). The court determined that this statutory language showed that Congress's "obvious intention . . . was to cut off all access to the databases for any reason." *City of Chicago v. Department of the Treasury,* 423 F.3d 777, 780 (7th Cir. 2005).

The second case, *City of New York v. Beretta U.S.A. Corp.,* 222 F.R.D. 51 (E.D. N.Y. 2004), concerned access to firearms information that was subject to the same appropriations language for fiscal year 2004 in Public Law 108-199.[60a] In this case, the demand for access took the form of subpoenas seeking discovery of the records in a tort suit by the City of New York and others against firearms manufacturers and distributors. The court in *City of New York* denied the agency's motion to quash the subpoenas, which was based largely on the appropriations language. The court held that the appropriations language, which prohibited public disclosure, was inapplicable by its terms since discovery could be accomplished under a protective order that would keep the records confidential. *City of New York,* 222 F.R.D. at 56–65.

Page 2-69 – Insert the following as new footnote 60a:

[60a] The litigation did not address whether the provisions were to be read as temporary or permanent. B-309704, Aug. 28, 2007, at 2 n.1.

D. Statutory Interpretation: Determining Congressional Intent

1. The Goal of Statutory Construction

Page 2-74 – Insert the following after the first full paragraph:

Of course, there are those rare occasions when two statutory provisions are just irreconcilable. Even then there is a statutory construction principle called the "last-in-time" rule. For example, in B-303268, Jan. 3, 2005, at issue was what Congress intended in enacting a "notwithstanding" clause in the State Department's fiscal year 2004 appropriations. Congress had appropriated a lump sum of $35 million to the Economic Support Fund for assistance to Lebanon, available "notwithstanding any other provision of law." Pub. L. No. 108-7, div. E, title V, § 534(a), 117 Stat. 11, 193 (Feb. 20,

2003). Five months earlier, in the 2003 Foreign Relations Authorization Act, Congress had included a provision, "notwithstanding any other provision of law," restricting from obligation $10 million "made available in fiscal year 2003 or any subsequent fiscal year" to the Economic Support Fund for assistance to Lebanon until the President submitted certain findings to Congress. Pub. L. No. 107-228, § 1224, 116 Stat. 1350, 1432 (Sept. 30, 2002). The two "notwithstanding" clauses presented an irreconcilable conflict that GAO resolved by applying the "last-in-time" rule of construction—that is, we presume that the later-enacted statute represents Congress's current expression of the law (*i.e.,* Congress's "last word"). Consequently, the "notwithstanding" clause of the appropriation act superseded the authorization act's "notwithstanding" clause. However, in this case the appropriation act's "notwithstanding" clause had effect only for fiscal year 2004. The authorization act's clause was permanent law. Thus the appropriation act's clause superseded the authorization act's clause *only* for fiscal year 2004, unless similar appropriation act provisions were enacted for subsequent fiscal years.

2. The "Plain Meaning" Rule

Page 2-74 – Replace the second full paragraph with the following:

By far the most important rule of statutory construction is this: You start with the language of the statute. Countless judicial decisions reiterate this rule. *E.g., BedRoc Limited, LLC v. United States,* 541 U.S. 176 (2004); *Lamie v. United States Trustee,* 540 U.S. 526 (2004); *Hartford Underwriters Insurance Co. v. Union Planters Bank, N.A.,* 530 U.S. 1 (2000); *Robinson v. Shell Oil Co.,* 519 U.S. 337 (1997); *Connecticut National Bank v. Germain,* 503 U.S. 249 (1992); *Mallard v. United States District Court for the Southern District of Iowa,* 490 U.S. 296, 300 (1989). The primary vehicle for Congress to express its intent is the words it enacts into law. As stated in an early Supreme Court decision: "The law as it passed is the will of the majority of both houses, and the only mode in which that will is spoken is in the act itself; and we must gather their intention from the language there used." *Aldridge v. Williams,* 44 U.S. (3 How.) 9, 24 (1845). A somewhat better known statement is from *United States v. American Trucking Ass'ns,* 310 U.S. 534, 543 (1940): "There is, of course, no more persuasive evidence of the purpose of a statute than the words by which the legislature undertook to give expression to its wishes."

Page 2-76 – Insert the following after the last paragraph:

Whether the language of the statute is sufficiently ambiguous that a court should look beyond it to legislative history can be difficult to discern. In *Zuni Public School District No. 89 v. Department of Education,* ___ U.S. , 127 S. Ct. 1534 (2007), the Court was faced with interpreting statutory language setting out a formula to be used by the Department of Education in connection with state funding of school districts. In a 5–4 decision, a majority of the court found the language in the statute to be sufficiently ambiguous to permit it to consider other indicators of congressional intent. The majority acknowledged that if the intent of Congress was clearly and unambiguously expressed by the statutory language, that would be the end of the Court's analysis.

3. The Limits of Literalism: Errors in Statutes and "Absurd Consequences"

Page 2-80 – Insert the following after the first paragraph:

The Supreme Court's recent decision in *Lamie v. United States Trustee,* 540 U.S. 526 (2004), contained an interesting discussion of drafting errors and what to do about them. For reasons that are described at length in the opinion but need not be repeated here, the Court found an "apparent legislative drafting error" in a 1994 statute. *Lamie,* 540 U.S. at 530. Nevertheless, the Court held that the amended language must be applied according to its plain terms. While the Court in *Lamie* acknowledged that the amended statute was awkward and ungrammatical, and that a literal reading rendered some words superfluous and could produce harsh results, none of these defects made the language ambiguous. *Id.* at 534–36. The Court determined that these flaws did not "lead to absurd results requiring us to treat the text as if it were ambiguous." *Id.* at 536. The Court also drew a distinction between construing a statute in a way that, in effect, added missing words as opposed to ignoring words that might have been included by mistake. *Id.* at 538.

Page 2-82 – Insert the following after the third paragraph:

Recent Supreme Court decisions likewise reinforce the need for caution when it comes to departing from statutory language on the basis of its apparent "absurd consequences." *See Lamie v. United States Trustee,* 540 U.S. 526, 537–38 (2004) ("harsh" consequences are not the equivalent of absurd consequences); *Barnhart v. Thomas,* 540 U.S. 20, 28–29 (2003) ("undesirable" consequences are not the equivalent of absurd consequences).

4. Statutory Aids to Construction

Page 2-84 – Replace the first full paragraph with the following:

Occasionally, the courts use the Dictionary Act to assist in resolving questions of interpretation. *E.g., Gonzalez v. Secretary for the Department of Corrections,* 366 F.3d 1253, 1263–64 (11th Cir. 2004) (applying the Dictionary Act's general rule that "words importing the singular include and apply to several persons, parties, or things," 1 U.S.C. § 1); *United States v. Reid,* 206 F. Supp. 2d 132

(D. Mass. 2002) (an aircraft is not a "vehicle" for purposes of the USA PATRIOT Act); *United States v. Belgarde,* 148 F. Supp. 2d 1104 (D. Mont.), *aff'd,* 300 F.3d 1177 (9th Cir. 2002) (a government agency, which the defendant was charged with burglarizing, is not a "person" for purposes of the Major Crimes Act). Courts also hold on occasion that the Dictionary Act does not apply. *See Rowland v. California Men's Colony,* 506 U.S.

194 (1993) (context refutes application of the title 1, United States Code, definition of "person"); *United States v. Ekanem,* 383 F.3d 40 (2nd Cir. 2004) ("victim" as used in the Mandatory Victims Restitution Act (MVRA) is not limited by the default definition of "person" in the Dictionary Act since that definition does not apply where context of MVRA indicates otherwise).

Page 2-84 – Replace the last paragraph with the following:

Congress regularly passes laws that "codify," or enact into positive law, the contents of various titles of the United States Code. The effect of such codifications is to make that United States Code title the official evidence of the statutory language it contains.[74] Codification acts typically delete obsolete provisions and make other technical and clarifying changes to the statutes they codify. Codification acts usually include language stating that they should not be construed as making substantive changes in the laws they replace. *See, e.g.,* Pub. L. No. 97-258, § 4(a), 96 Stat. 877, 1067 (1982) (codifying title 31 of the United States Code). *See also Scheidler v. National Organization for Women,* 547 U.S. 9 (2006); 69 Comp. Gen. 691 (1990).[75]

5. Canons of Statutory Construction

Page 2-86 – Replace the first full paragraph with the following:

Like all other courts, the Supreme Court follows this venerable canon.

E.g., United States v. Cleveland Indians Baseball Co., 532 U.S. 200, 217 (2001) ("it is, of course, true that statutory construction 'is a holistic endeavor' and that the meaning of a provision is 'clarified by the remainder of the statutory scheme'"); *FDA v. Brown and Williamson Tobacco Corp.*, 529 U.S. 120 (2000); *Gustafson v. Alloyd Co., Inc.*, 513 U.S. 561, 569 (1995) ("the Act is to be interpreted as a symmetrical and coherent regulatory scheme, one in which the operative words have a consistent meaning throughout"); *Brown v. Gardner,* 513 U.S. 115, 118 (1994) ("[a]mbiguity is a creature not of definitional possibilities but of statutory context"). *See also Hibbs v. Winn,* 542 U.S. 88, 101 (2004) (courts should construe a statute so that "effect is given to all its provisions, so that no part will be inoperative or superfluous, void or insignificant"); *General Dynamics Land Systems, Inc. v. Cline,* 540 U.S. 581, 598 (2004) (courts should not ignore "the cardinal rule that statutory language must be read in context since a phrase gathers meaning from the words around it").

Page 2-87 – Add the following bullet to the first full paragraph and revise the second bullet as follows:

- B-302335, Jan. 15, 2004: When read as a whole, the Emergency Steel Loan Guarantee Act of 1999, 15 U.S.C. § 1841 note, clearly appropriated loan guarantee programs funds to the Loan Guarantee Board and not the Department of Commerce.
- B-303961, Dec. 6, 2004: Despite use of the phrase "notwithstanding any other provision of law" in a provision of an appropriation act, nothing in the statute read as a whole or its legislative history suggested an intended waiver of the Antideficiency Act. See also B-290125.2, B-290125.3, Dec. 18, 2002 (redacted) (viewed in isolation, the phrase "notwithstanding any other provision of law" might be read as exempting a procurement from GAO's bid protest jurisdiction under the Competition in Contracting Act; however, when the statute is read as a whole, as it must be, it does not exempt the procurement from the Act).

Page 2-88 – Add the following bullets to the first paragraph:

- *Hibbs v. Winn,* 542 U.S. 88, 101 (2004): "The rule against superfluities complements the principle that courts are to interpret the words of a statute in context."
- *Alaska Department of Environmental Conservation v. EPA,* 540 U.S. 461, 489 n.13 (2004): A statute should be construed so that, "if it can be prevented, no clause, sentence, or word shall be superfluous, void, or insignificant."

Page 2-88 – Replace the last paragraph as follows:

Although frequently invoked, the no surplusage canon is less absolute than the "whole statute" canon. One important caveat, previously discussed, is that words in a statute will be treated as surplus and disregarded if they were included in error. *E.g., Chickasaw Nation v. United States,* 534 U.S. 84, 94 (2001) (emphasis in original): "The canon requiring a court to give effect to each word '*if possible*' is sometimes offset by the canon that permits a court to reject words 'as surplusage' if 'inadvertently inserted or if repugnant to the rest of the statute.'" Citing *Chickasaw Nation,* the Court also recently observed that the canon of avoiding surplusage will not be invoked to create ambiguity in a statute that has a plain meaning if the language in question is disregarded. *Lamie v. United States Trustee,* 540 U.S. 526, 536 (2004).

Page 2-89 – Replace the first and second paragraphs with the following:

When words used in a statute are not specifically defined, they are generally given their "plain" or ordinary meaning rather than some obscure usage. *E.g., Engine Manufacturers Ass'n v. South Coast Air Quality Management District,* 541 U.S. 246 (2004); *BedRoc Limited, LLC v. United States,* 541 U.S. 176 (2004); *Asgrow Seed Co. v. Winterboer,* 513 U.S. 179, 187 (1995); *Federal Deposit Insurance Corp. v. Meyer,* 510 U.S. 471, 476 (1994); *Mallard v. United States,* 490 U.S. 296, 301 (1989); B-261193, Aug. 25, 1995; 70 Comp. Gen. 705 (1991); 38 Comp. Gen. 812 (1959).

One commonsense way to determine the plain meaning of a word is to consult a dictionary. *E.g., Mallard,* 490 U.S. at 301; *American Mining Congress v. EPA,* 824 F.2d 1177, 1183–84 and n. 7 (D.C. Cir. 1987). Thus, the Comptroller General relied on the dictionary in B-251189, Apr. 8, 1993, to hold that business suits did not constitute "uniforms," which would have permitted the use of appropriated funds for their purchase. *See also* B-302973, Oct. 6, 2004; B-261522, Sept. 29, 1995.

Page 2-90 – Replace the second full paragraph with the following:

Several different canons of construction revolve around these seemingly straightforward notions. Before discussing some of them, it is important to note once more that these canons, like most others, may or may not make sense to apply in particular settings. Indeed, the basic canon that the same words have the same meaning in a statute is itself subject to exceptions. In *Cleveland Indians Baseball Club,* the Court cautioned: "Although we generally presume that identical words used in different parts of the same act are intended to have the same meaning, … the presumption is not rigid, and the meaning [of the same words] well may vary with the purposes of the law." *Cleveland Indians Baseball Club,* 532 U.S. at 213 (citations and quotation marks omitted). To drive the point home, the Court quoted the following admonition from a law review article:

> "The tendency to assume that a word which appears in two or more legal rules, and so in connection with more than one purpose, has and should have precisely the same scope in all of them … has all the tenacity of original sin and must constantly be guarded against."

Id. See also General Dynamics Land Systems, Inc. v. Cline, 540 U.S. 581, 594–96 and fn. 8 (2004) (quoting the same law review passage, which it notes "has become a staple of our opinions"). Of course, all bets are off if the statute clearly uses the same word differently in different places. See Robinson v. Shell Oil Co., 519 U.S. 337, 343 (1997) ("[o]nce it is established that the term 'employees' includes former employees in some sections, but not in others, the term standing alone is necessarily ambiguous").

Page 2-90 – Insert the following before the last partial paragraph:

In 2007, the Court applied the exception described in the Cleveland Indians Baseball Club case in Environmental Defense v. Duke Energy Corp., ___ U.S. ___, 127 S. Ct. 1423 (2007) (upholding differing regulatory definitions of the same statutory term contained in two sections of the Clean Air Act). Rejecting the lower court's holding that there is an "effectively irrebuttable" presumption that the same defined term in different provisions of the same statute must be "interpreted identically," the Court pointed out simply that "[c]ontext counts." Id. at 1433.

Page 2-93 – Replace the first full paragraph with the following:

Likewise, a statute's grammatical structure is useful but not conclusive.

Lamie v. United States Trustee, 540 U.S. 526, 534–35 (2004) (the mere fact that a statute is awkwardly worded or even ungrammatical does not make it ambiguous). Nevertheless, the Court sometimes gives significant weight to the grammatical structure of a statute. For example, in Barnhart v. Thomas, 540 U.S. 20, 26 (2003), the Court rejected the lower court's construction of a statute in part because it violated the grammatical "rule of the last antecedent." Also, in Arcadia, Ohio v. Ohio Power Co., 498 U.S. 73 (1991), the Court devoted considerable attention to the placement of the word "or" in a series of clauses. It questioned the interpretation proffered by one of the parties that would have given the language an awkward effect, noting: "In casual conversation, perhaps, such absentminded duplication and omission are possible, but Congress is not presumed to draft its laws that way."

Arcadia, 498 U.S. at 79. By contrast, in Nobelman v. American Savings Bank, 508 U.S. 324, 330 (1993), the Court rejected an interpretation, noting: "We acknowledge that this reading of the clause is quite sensible as a matter of grammar. But it is not compelled."

Page 2-94 – Replace the first full paragraph with the following:

The same considerations apply to a statute's popular name and to the headings, or titles, of particular sections of the statute. See Intel Corp. v. Advanced Micro Devices, Inc., 542 U.S. 241, 242 (2004) ("A statute's caption . . . cannot undo or limit its text's plain meaning").

See also Immigration and Naturalization Service v. St. Cyr, 533 U.S. 289, 308–09 (2001); Pennsylvania Department of Corrections v. Yeskey, 524 U.S. 206, 212 (1998). In St. Cyr, the Supreme Court concluded that a section entitled "Elimination of Custody Review by Habeas Corpus" did not, in fact, eliminate habeas corpus jurisdiction. It found that the substantive terms of the section were less definitive than the title. See also McConnell v. Federal Election Commission, 540 U.S. 93, 180 (2003).

Page 2-94 – Replace the second full paragraph with the following:

Preambles. Federal statutes often include an introductory "preamble" or "purpose" section before the substantive provisions in which Congress sets forth findings, purposes, or policies that prompted it to adopt the legislation. Such preambles have no legally binding effect. However, they may provide indications of congressional intent underlying the law. Sutherland states with respect to preambles:

> "[T]he settled principle of law is that the preamble cannot control the enacting part of the statute in cases where the enacting part is expressed in clear, unambiguous terms. In case any doubt arises in the enacted part, the preamble may be resorted to to help discover the intention of the law maker."

2A Sutherland, § 47:04 at 221–22.[80] For a recent example in which the Court used statutory findings to inform its interpretation of congressional intent, see *General Dynamics Land Systems, Inc. v Cline,* 540 U.S. 581, 589–91 (2004).

6. Legislative History

Page 2-96 – Replace footnote number 81 with the following:

[81] The majority opinion in *Association of American Physicians and Surgeons* placed heavy reliance on *Public Citizen,* noting that "[t]he Court

adopted, we think it is fair to say, an extremely strained construction of the word 'utilized' in order to avoid the constitutional question." *Association of American Physicians and Surgeons,* 997 F.2d at 906. Both *Public Citizen* and *Association of American Physicians and Surgeons* drew strongly worded concurring opinions along the same lines. The concurring opinions maintained that FACA clearly applied by its plain terms to the respective groups, but that its application was unconstitutional as so applied. The District of Columbia Circuit Court of Appeals clarified its holding in *American Physicians and Surgeons* in 2005. *In re Cheney*,. 406 F.3d 723 (D.C. Cir. 2005). There, in order to avoid "severe separation-of-powers problems" in applying FACA on the basis that private parties were involved with a committee in the Executive Office of the President, the court held that for purposes of FACA "a committee is composed wholly of federal officials if the President has given no one other than a federal official a vote in or, if the committee acts by consensus, a veto over the committee's decisions." *Id.* at 728.

Page 2-97 – Replace the second full paragraph with the following:

The use becomes improper when the line is crossed from using legislative history to resolve things that are not clear in the statutory language to using it to rewrite the statute. *E.g., Shannon v. United States,* 512 U.S. 573, 583 (1994) (declining to give effect to "a single passage of legislative history that is no way anchored in the text of the statute"); *Ratzlaf v. United States,* 510 U.S. 135, 147–48 (1994) (declining to "resort to legislative history to cloud a statutory text that is clear"); *Brill v. Countrywide Home Loans, Inc.*, 427 F.3d 446, 448 (7th Cir. 2005) (noting that "when the legislative history stands by itself, as a naked expression of 'intent' unconnected to any enacted text, it has no more force than an opinion poll of legislators—less, really, as it speaks for fewer"). The Comptroller General put it this way:

Page 2-99 – Replace the second full paragraph with the following:

However, material in committee reports, even a conference report, will ordinarily not be used to controvert clear statutory language. *Squillacote,* 739 F.2d at 1218; *Hart v. United States,* 585 F.2d 1025 (Ct. Cl. 1978); B-278121, Nov. 7, 1997; B-33911, B-62187, July 15, 1948. Also, it will not be used to add requirements that Congress did not include in the statute itself. For example, where Congress appropriates lump sum amounts without statutorily restricting the use of those funds, "a clear inference arises that it does not intend to impose legally binding restrictions, and indicia in committee reports and other legislative history as to how the funds should or are expected to be spent do not establish any legal requirements" on the agency. 55 Comp. Gen. 307, 319 (1975); *see also Hein v. Freedom From Religion Foundation, Inc.*, ___ U.S. ___, 127 S. Ct. 2553, 2568 n.7 (2007); *Lincoln v. Vigil,* 508 U.S. 182, 192 (1993). Also, such material is not entitled to any weight as legislative history if the statement in the report is unrelated to any language in the act itself. *Abrego Abrego v. Dow Chemical Co.*, 443 F.3d 676 (9th Cir. 2006); *Brill v. Countrywide Home Loans, Inc.*, 427 F.3d 446 (7th Cir. 2005).

An interesting example of the weight accorded report language which alters the plain meaning and effect of the statutory language is in *Arlington Central School District Board of Education v. Murphy,* 548 U.S. ___, 126 S. Ct. 2455 (2006). In this case the issue was whether a provision of the Individuals with Disabilities Education Act (IDEA) authorizing the award of attorney fees and costs to parents who prevailed in lawsuits under the act extended to costs incurred for experts. The Court approached the issue by noting that the conditions Congress attaches to the receipt of federal funds by states are contractual in nature and must therefore be expressed "unambiguously" in order to give states adequate notice of what they are accepting. *Arlington Central,* 126 S. Ct. at 2459. It went on to hold that the IDEA statute did not clearly indicate that expert fees were covered by its fee-shifting provision. On the contrary, the Court concluded that the language of the fee-shifting provision and other IDEA provisions strongly suggested that expert fees were not covered. The Court was influenced by the judicial rule that the term "costs" in fee-shifting provisions is a term of art that generally does not include expert fees. *Id.* The most striking aspect of the Court's opinion was its rejection of legislative history from the conference report that explicitly stated the intent to include expert costs in IDEA's fee-shifting provision. The conference report, quoted in the opinion at 126 S. Ct. 2463, could not have been clearer: "The conferees intend that the term 'attorneys' fees as part of the costs' include reasonable expenses and fees of expert witnesses and the reasonable costs of any test or evaluation which is found to be necessary for the preparation of the . . . case." Nevertheless, the Court concluded:

> "Whatever weight this legislative history would merit in another context, it is not sufficient here. Putting the legislative history aside, we see virtually no support for respondents' position. Under these circumstances, where everything other than the legislative history overwhelmingly suggests that expert fees may not be recovered, the legislative history is simply not enough."

Id. Thus, the conference report statement could not make up for the absence of any statutory language making expert fees reimbursable. Cf. B-307767, Nov. 13, 2006 (floor statement is not entitled to weight as legislative history when the statute is clear on its face since the statement provides an individual member's views and does not necessarily represent the meaning and purpose of the lawmaking body collectively).

Page 2-102 – Replace the first full paragraph with the following:

Statements by the sponsor of a bill are also entitled to somewhat more weight. E.g., Schwegmann Brothers v. Calvert Distillers Corp., 341 U.S. 384, 394–95 (1951); Ex Parte Kawato, 317 U.S. 69, 77 (1942). However, they are not controlling. General Dynamics Land Systems, Inc. v. Cline, 540 U.S. 581, 597–99 (2004); Chrysler Corp. v. Brown, 441 U.S. 281, 311 (1979).

Page 2-104 – Replace the last paragraph with the following:

GAO naturally follows the principle that post-enactment statements do not constitute legislative history. E.g., 72 Comp. Gen. 317 (1993); 54 Comp. Gen. 819, 822 (1975). Likewise, the Office of Legal Counsel has virtually conceded that presidential signing statements fall within the realm of post-enactment statements that carry no weight as legislative history. See 17 Op. Off. Legal Counsel 131 (1993).[85] In 2007, GAO examined how the federal courts have treated signing statements in their published decisions. A search of all federal case law since 1945 found fewer than 140 cases that cited presidential signing statements, most commonly to supplement legislative history such as committee reports. Courts also have cited signing statements to establish the date of signing, provide a short summary of the statute, explain the purpose of the statute, or describe the underlying policy behind the statute. GAO concluded that, overall, federal courts infrequently cite or refer to signing statements in their published opinions. B-308603, June 18, 2007, Enclosure IV. See also B-309928,. Dec. 20, 2007, for additional discussion on signing statements.

Page 2-105 – Replace footnote 85 with the following:

[85] While this opinion stopped short of attempting "finally to decide" the matter, it presented several powerful arguments against the validity of signing statements as legislative history but no arguments in favor of their use for this purpose. On June 27, 2006, the Senate Judiciary Committee held a hearing on the subject of presidential signing statements. Background on the hearing, including witness statements, can be found at http://judiciary.senate.gov/hearing.cfm?id=1969 (last visited Feb. 8, 2008).

Page 2-105 – Add the following to the third full paragraph:

- Doe v. Chao, 540 U.S. 614, 621–23 (2004): Congress deleted from the bill language that would have provided for the type of damage award sought by the petitioner. See also F. Hoffman-La Roche Ltd v. Empagran S.A., 542 U.S. 155 (2004); Resolution Trust Corp. v. Gallagher, 10 F.3d 416 423. (7th Cir. 1993); *Davis v. United States*, 46 Fed. Cl. 421 (2000).

7. Presumptions and "Clear Statement" Rules

Page 2-113 – Replace the first full paragraph with the following:

There is a strong presumption against waiver of the federal government's immunity from suit. The courts have repeatedly held that waivers of sovereign immunity must be "unequivocally expressed." *E.g., United States v. Nordic Village, Inc.,* 503 U.S. 30 (1992); *Marathon Oil Co. v. United States,* 374 F.3d 1123, 1127 (Fed. Cir. 2004), *cert. denied,* 544 U.S. 1031 (2005); *Shoshone Indian Tribe of the Wind River Reservation, Wyoming v. United States,* 51 Fed. Cl. 60 (2001), *aff'd,* 364 F.3d 1339 (Fed. Cir. 2004), *cert. denied,* 544 U.S. 973 (2005). Legislative history does not help for this purpose. The relevant statutory language in *Nordic Village* was ambiguous and could have been read, evidently with the support of the legislative history, to impose monetary liability on the United States. The Court rejected such a reading, applying instead the same approach as described above in its federalism jurisprudence:

> "[L]egislative history has no bearing on the ambiguity point. As in the Eleventh Amendment context, see *Hoffman, supra,* ... the 'unequivocal expression' of elimination of sovereign immunity that we insist upon is an expression in statutory text. If clarity does not exist there, it cannot be supplied by a committee report."
>
> *Nordic Village,* 503 U.S. at 37.

Chapter 3

AGENCY REGULATIONS AND ADMINISTRATIVE DISCRETION

A. AGENCY REGULATIONS

Page 3-2 – Replace the second paragraph with the following:

As a conceptual starting point, agency regulations fall into three broad categories. First, every agency head has the authority, largely inherent but also authorized generally by 5 U.S.C. § 301,[1] to issue regulations to govern the internal affairs of the agency. Regulations in this category may include such subjects as conflicts of interest, employee travel, and delegations to organizational components. This statute is nothing more than a grant of authority for what are called "housekeeping" regulations. *Chrysler Corp. v. Brown,* 441 U.S. 281, 309 (1979); *Smith v. Cromer,* 159 F.3d 875, 878 (4th Cir. 1998), *cert. denied,* 528 U.S. 826 (1999); *NLRB v. Capitol Fish Co.,* 294 F.2d 868, 875 (5th Cir. 1961). It confers "administrative power only."

United States v. George, 228 U.S. 14, 20 (1913); B-302582, Sept. 30, 2004;

54 Comp. Gen. 624, 626 (1975). Thus, the statute merely grants agencies authority to issue regulations that govern their own internal affairs; it does not authorize rulemaking that creates substantive legal rights. *Schism v. United States,* 316 F.3d 1259, 1278–84 (Fed. Cir. 2002), *cert. denied,* 539 U.S. 910 (2003).

1. The Administrative Procedure Act

Page 3-6 – Replace the cite after the quoted language carried over from page 3-5 with the following paragraph:

Richard J. Pierce, Jr., *Administrative Law Treatise,* § 7.4 at 442 (4th ed. 2000) (citations omitted). Two decisions make clear that the courts will insist upon at least some ascertainable and coherent rationale: *Northeast Maryland Waste Disposal Authority v. EPA,* 358 F.3d 936, 948 (D.C. Cir. 2004) (the court remanded a rule to the agency because it was "frankly, stunned to find" that the agency had provided "*not one word* in the proposed or final rule" (emphasis in original) to explain a key aspect of its rule), and *International Union, United Mine Workers of America v. Department of Labor,* 358 F.3d 40, 45 (D.C. Cir. 2004) (finding that the agency's stated rationale to withdraw a proposed rule was disjointed and conclusory, the court returned the matter to the agency "so that it may either proceed with the . . . rulemaking or give a reasoned account of its decision not to do so").

Page 3-9 – Replace the second full paragraph with the following:

As a starting point, anything that falls within the definition of a "rule" in 5 U.S.C. § 551(4) and for which formal rulemaking is not required, is subject to the informal rulemaking procedures of 5 U.S.C. § 553 unless exempt. This statement is not as encompassing as it may seem, since section 553 itself provides several very significant exemptions. These exemptions, according to a line of decisions by the U.S. Court of Appeals for the District of Columbia Circuit, will be "narrowly construed and only reluctantly countenanced." *Jifry v. Federal Aviation Administration,* 370 F.3d 1174, 1179 (D.C. Cir. 2004), *cert. denied,* 543 U.S. 1146 (2005); *Utility Solid Waste Activities Group v. EPA,* 236 F.3d 749, 754 (D.C. Cir. 2001); *Asiana Airlines v. Federal Aviation Administration,*. 134 F.3d 393, 396–97 (D.C. Cir. 1998); *Tennessee Gas Pipeline Co. v. Federal Energy Regulatory Commission,* 969 F.2d 1141, 1144 (D.C. Cir. 1992); *New Jersey Department of Environmental Protection v. EPA,* 626 F.2d 1038, 1045 (D.C. Cir. 1980).[8] Be that as it may, they appear in the statute and cannot be disregarded. For example, section 553 does not apply to matters "relating to agency management or personnel or to public property, loans, grants, benefits, or contracts." 5 U.S.C. § 553(a)(2).

Page 3-9 – Replace footnote 8 with the following:

[8] In *Utility Solid Waste Activities Group,* 236 F.3d at 754–55, the court held that the "good cause" exemption in section 553(b) does not allow an agency to forego notice and comment when correcting a technical error in a regulation. Likewise, the court held that agencies have no "inherent power"

to correct such technical errors outside of the APA procedures. *Id.* at 752–54. The decision in *Jifry* provides an example of a case upholding an agency's use of the good cause exemption based on emergency conditions involving potential security threats. *Jifry,* 370 F.3d at 1179.

4. Waiver of Regulations

Page 3-21 – Replace the first full paragraph with the following:

Sometimes legislative regulations or the statutes they implement do explicitly authorize "waivers" in certain circumstances. Here, of course, the waiver authority is an integral part of the underlying statutory or regulatory scheme. Accordingly, courts give effect to such waiver provisions and, indeed, they may even hold that an agency's failure to consider or permit waiver is an abuse of discretion. However, the courts usually accord considerable deference to agency decisions on whether or not to grant discretionary waivers. For illustrative cases, see *BDPCS, Inc. v. FCC,* 351 F.3d 1177 (D.C. Cir. 2003); *People of the State of New York and Public Service Commission of the State of New York v. FCC,* 267 F.3d 91 (2nd Cir. 2001); *BellSouth Corporation v. FCC,* 162 F.3d 1215 (D.C. Cir. 1999); *Rauenhorst v. United States Department of Transportation,* 95 F.3d 715 (8th Cir. 1996).

B. AGENCY ADMINISTRATIVE INTERPRETATIONS

1. Interpretation of Statutes

Page 3-29 – Replace the second full paragraph with the following:

In what is now recognized as one of the key cases in determining how much "deference" is due an agency interpretation, *Chevron, Inc. v. Natural Resources Defense Council,* 467 U.S. 837 (1984), the Court formulated its approach to deference in terms of two questions. The first question is "whether Congress has directly spoken to the precise question at issue." *Id.* at 842. If it has, the agency must of course comply with clear congressional intent, and regulations to the contrary will be invalidated. Thus, before you ever get to questions of deference, it must first be determined that the regulation is not contrary to the statute, a question of delegated authority rather than deference. "If a court, employing traditional tools of statutory construction, ascertains that Congress had an intention on the precise question at issue, that intention is the law and must be given effect." *Id.* at 843 n.9. An example is *General Dynamics Land Systems, Inc. v. Cline,* 540 U.S. 581 (2004), in which the Court declined to give *Chevron* deference, or any lesser degree of deference, to an agency interpretation that it found to be "clearly wrong" as a matter of statutory construction, since the agency interpretation was contrary to the act's text, structure, purpose, history, and relationship to other federal statutes.

Page 3-30 – Replace the second full paragraph with the following and insert new footnote number 30a as follows:

When the agency's interpretation is in the form of a regulation with the force and effect of law, the deference, as we have seen, is at its highest.[30] The agency's position is entitled to *Chevron* deference and should be upheld unless it is arbitrary or capricious. There should be no question of substitution of judgment.[30a] If the agency position can be said to be reasonable or to have a rational basis within the statutory grant of authority, it should stand, even though the reviewing body finds some other position preferable. *See, e.g., Household Credit Services, Inc. v. Pfennig,* 541 U.S. 232 (2004); *Barnhart v. Thomas,* 540 U.S. 20 (2003); *Yellow Transportation, Inc. v. Michigan,* 537 U.S. 36 (2002); *Shalala v. Illinois Council on Long Term Care, Inc.,* 529 U.S. 1, 20–21 (2000); *American Telephone and Telegraph Corp. v. Iowa Utility Board,* 525 U.S. 366 (1999). *Chevron* deference is also given to authoritative agency positions in formal adjudication. *See Immigration and Naturalization Service v. Aguirre-Aguirre,* 526 U.S. 415 (1999) (holding that a Bureau of Indian Affairs statutory interpretation developed in case-by-case formal adjudication should be accorded *Chevron* deference). For an extensive list of Supreme Court cases giving *Chevron* deference to agency statutory interpretations found in rulemaking or formal adjudication, see *United States v. Mead Corp.,* 533 U.S. 218, 231 at n.12 (2001).

Page 3-30 – Insert the following for new footnote number 30a:

[30a] This is true even if the statute in question has been construed previously by a court, unless the court interpreted the statute according to "the unambiguous terms of the statute[, leaving] no room for agency discretion." *National Cable and Telecommunications Ass'n v. Brand X Internet Services,* 545 U.S. 967 (2005). This result stems from the policy underlying *Chevron* deference, that is, the presumption that Congress, when it leaves ambiguity in a statute, means for the agency to resolve the ambiguity, exercising whatever degree of discretion the ambiguity allows. "[I]t is for agencies, not courts, to fill statutory gaps." *Id.*

Page 3-32 – Replace the third bulleted paragraph with the following:

- Evidence (or lack thereof) of congressional awareness of, and acquiescence in, the administrative position. United States v. American Trucking Ass'n, 310 U.S. 534, 549–50 (1940); Helvering v. Winmill, 305 U.S. 79, 82–83 (1938); Norwegian Nitrogen Products Co. v. United States, 288 U.S. 294, 313–15 (1933); Collins v. United States, 946 F.2d 864 (Fed. Cir. 1991); Davis v. Director, Office of Workers' Compensation Programs, Department of Labor, 936 F.2d 1111, 1115–16 (10th Cir. 1991); 41 Op. Att'y Gen. 57 (1950); B-114829-O.M., July 17, 1974. Interestingly, in Coke v. Long Island Care At Home, Ltd., 376 F.3d 118 (2nd Cir. 2004), the court acknowledged the potential relevance of congressional acquiescence to a 30-year-old regulation, noting that Congress had amended the applicable statute seven times over the life of the regulation without expressing any disapproval of it. However, the court ultimately rejected the congressional acquiescence argument—according to the court, "affectionately known as the 'dog didn't bark canon'"—and held the regulation invalid. Id. at 130 and n.5.

Page 3-33 – Replace the first full paragraph with the following:

More recent decisions further indicate that *Chevron* deference may extend beyond legislative rules and formal adjudications. Most notably, the Supreme Court observed in *dicta* in *Barnhart v. Walton,* 535 U.S. at 222, that *Mead Corp.* "denied [any] suggestion" in *Christensen* that *Chevron* deference was limited to interpretations adopted through formal rulemaking. The *Barnhart* opinion went on to say that:

> "In this case, the interstitial nature of the legal question, the related expertise of the Agency, the importance of the question to the administration of the statute, the complexity of that administration, and the careful consideration the Agency has given the question over a long period of time all indicate that *Chevron* provides the appropriate legal lens through which to view the legality of the Agency interpretation here at issue."

Id. at 222.[33] See also General Dynamics Land Systems, Inc. v. Cline, 540 U.S. 581 (2004); Edelman v. Lynchburg College, 535 U.S. 106, 114 (2002). Two additional decisions are instructive in terms of the limits of Chevron. In both cases the Court found that the issuances containing agency statutory interpretations were entitled to some weight, but not Chevron deference. Raymond B. Yates, M.D., P.C., Profit Sharing Plan v. Hendon,

541 U.S. 1 (agency advisory opinion); Alaska Department of Environmental Conservation v. EPA, 540 U.S. 461 (2004) (internal agency guidance memoranda).

Page 3-33 – Replace the third full paragraph with the following:

Circuit court decisions have added to the confusion. See Coke v. Long Island Care at Home, Ltd., 376 F.3d 118 (2nd Cir. 2004) (the court found that a regulation was not entitled to Chevron deference, despite congressional acquiescence and even though the statute was ambiguous and the regulation was issued through notice and comment rulemaking, because evidence showed the agency intended the regulation to be only an "interpretive" as opposed to a "legislative" rule); Doe v. United States, 372 F.3d 1347, 1357–59 (Fed. Cir. 2004), cert. denied, 544 U.S. 904 (2005) (court applied Chevron deference to an Office of Personnel Management regulation issued under general rulemaking authority); James v. Von Zemenszky, 301 F.3d 1364 (Fed. Cir. 2002) (ignoring Barnhart factors because the agency statutory interpretation contained in a directive and handbook "f[e]ll within the class of informal agency interpretations that do not ordinarily merit Chevron deference"); Federal Election Commission v. National Rifle Ass'n, 254 F.3d 173 (D.C. Cir. 2001) (holding that Federal Election Committee (FEC) advisory opinions are entitled to Chevron deference); Matz v. Household International Tax Reduction Investment Plan, 265 F.3d 572 (7th Cir. 2001) (holding that an Internal Revenue Service (IRS) statutory interpretation in an amicus brief, supported by an IRS Revenue Ruling and agency manual, was not entitled to Chevron deference); Klinedinst v. Swift Investments, Inc., 260 F.3d 1251 (11th Cir. 2001) (holding that a Department of Labor handbook was not due Chevron deference); TeamBank v. McClure, 279 F.3d 614 (8th Cir. 2002) (holding that Office of the Controller of the Currency informal adjudications are due Chevron deference); In re Sealed Case, 223 F.3d 775 (D.C. Cir. 2000) (holding that FEC's probable cause determinations are entitled to Chevron deference). As Professor Pierce notes:

> "After Mead, it is possible to know only that legislative rules and formal adjudications are always entitled to Chevron deference, while less formal pronouncements like interpretative rules and informal adjudications may or may not be entitled to Chevron deference. The deference due a less formal pronouncement seems to depend on the results of judicial application of an apparently open-ended list of factors that arguably qualify as 'other indication[s] of a comparable congressional intent' to give a particular type of agency pronouncement the force of law."34

Page 3-35 – Replace the last paragraph with the following:

The deference principle does not apply to an agency's interpretation of a statute that is not part of its program or enabling legislation or is a statute of general applicability. *See Adams v. SEC,* 287 F.3d 183 (D.C. Cir. 2002); *Contractor's Sand and Gravel v. Federal Mine Safety and Health Commission,* 199 F.3d 1335 (D.C. Cir. 2000); *Association of Civilian Technicians v. Federal Labor Relations Authority,* 200 F.3d 590. (9th Cir. 2000). In "split-jurisdiction" situations, where multiple agencies share specific statutory responsibility, courts have determined that *Chevron* deference is due to the primary executive branch enforcer and the agency accountable for overall administration of the statutory scheme. *See Martin v. Occupational Safety and Health Review Commission,* 499 U.S. 144 (1991); *Collins v. National Transportation Safety Board,* 351 F.3d 1246 (D.C. Cir. 2003).

2. Interpretation of Agency's Own Regulations

Page 3-38 – Insert the following new paragraph after the quote at the top of the page:

Recent cases according *Seminole Rock* deference to agency interpretations of their regulations include: *Entergy Services, Inc. v. Federal Energy Regulatory Commission,* 375 F.3d. 1204, 1209 (D.C. Cir. 2004); *Castlewood Products, L.L.C. v. Norton,* 365 F.3d 1076, 1079 (D.C. Cir. 2004); *In re Sullivan,* 362 F.3d 1324, 1328 (Fed. Cir. 2004). In *WHX Corp. v. SEC,* 362 F.3d 854, 860. (D.C. Cir. 2004), the court did not defer to an agency interpretation because the interpretation rested entirely on staff advice and there was no formal agency precedent or official interpretative guideline on point.

Page 3-39 – Insert the following after the last full paragraph:

Recently the Court held than an agency's interpretation of its own regulation is entitled to *Auer* deference only when the regulation interpreted is itself a product of the agency's expertise and authority in a given area. In *Gonzales v. Oregon,* 546 U.S. 243 (2006), the Court examined an interpretive rule issued by the Attorney General, which stated that assisting suicide was not a "legitimate medical purpose" for which doctors could prescribe drugs, and doctors doing so would violate the Controlled Substance Act (CSA). *Id.* at 254. The Attorney General argued that the rule was entitled to *Auer* deference because it interpreted the term "legitimate medical purpose" as that term was used in a 1971 regulation issued by the Attorney General under the CSA.

However, the Court found *Auer* deference unwarranted, because rather than reflecting the Attorney General's deliberation and imprimatur, the 1971 regulation merely mimicked the language of the CSA. The Court stated:

> "In *Auer,* the underlying regulations gave specificity to a statutory scheme . . . and reflected the considerable experience and expertise the Department of Labor had acquired over time with respect to the complexities of the [statutory scheme]. Here, on the other hand, the underlying regulation does little more than restate the terms of the statute itself. The language the Interpretive Rule addresses comes from Congress, not the Attorney General, and the near-equivalence of the statute and regulation belies the Government's argument for *Auer* deference."
>
> *Gonzales,* 546 U.S. at 256–57.

In contrast to some of the more muddled deference cases discussed previously, *Gonzales* draws a bright line when it comes to an agency's interpretation of its own regulation. "An agency does not acquire special authority to interpret its own words when, instead of using its expertise and experience to formulate a regulation, it has elected merely to paraphrase the statutory language." *Id.* at 257.

C. Administrative Discretion

1. Introduction

Page 3-41 – Replace the first full paragraph with the following:

Under the Administrative Procedure Act (APA), action that is "committed to agency discretion by law" is not subject to judicial review. 5 U.S.C. § 701(a)(2). As the Supreme Court has pointed out, this is a "very narrow exception" applicable in "rare instances" where, quoting from the APA's legislative history, "statutes are drawn in such broad terms that in a given case there is no law to apply." *Citizens to Preserve Overton Park, Inc. v. Volpe,* 401 U.S. 402, 410 (1971). As noted, the "no law to apply" exception is uncommon, and most exercises of discretion will be found reviewable at least to some extent.[37] *See Raymond Proffitt Foundation v. Corps of Engineers,* 343 F.3d 199, 207 (3rd Cir. 2003); *City of Los Angeles v. Department of Commerce,* 307 F.3d 859 (9th Cir. 2002); *Drake v. Federal*

Aviation Administration, 291 F.3d 59 (D.C. Cir. 2002), *cert. denied,.* 537 U.S. 1193 (2003); *Fox Television Stations, Inc. v. FCC,* 280 F.3d 1027 (D.C. Cir. 2002); *Diebold v. United States,* 947 F.2d 787 (6th Cir. 1991).

Page 3-41 – Replace footnote number 37 with the following:

[37] However, agency inaction in declining to initiate enforcement or other regulatory action is subject to "a presumption of unreviewability," although that presumption is rebuttable. *Heckler v. Chaney,* 470 U.S. 821 (1985). Another obvious exception is if a statute explicitly precludes judicial review. *See Jordan Hospital, Inc. v. Shalala,* 276 F.3d 72 (1st Cir.), *cert. denied,* 537 U.S. 812 (2002); *National Coalition to Save Our Mall v. Norton,* 269 F.3d 1092 (D.C. Cir. 2001), *cert. denied,* 537 U.S. 813 (2002) (construction of World War II memorial); *Ismailov v. Reno,* 263 F.3d 851 (8th Cir. 2001) (refusal to extend deadline for asylum application). *See also Ohio Public Interest Research Group, Inc. v. Whitman,.* 386 F.3d 792 (6th Cir. 2004); *Godwin v. Secretary of Housing and Urban Development,* 356 F.3d 310 (D.C. Cir. 2004).

Page 3-42 – Insert the following new paragraphs after the last bulleted paragraph:

Even where the APA does not flatly preclude judicial review, the courts will entertain a lawsuit under the Act only if it involves an "agency action" that is subject to redress under the Act. In *Norton v. Southern Utah Wilderness Alliance,* 542 U.S. 55 (2004), the Court rejected a suit under the APA to compel the Interior Department to regulate the use of off-road vehicles on certain federal wilderness lands. The Court concluded that there was no legal mandate requiring the agency to take such action. The Court described the jurisdictional parameters of the APA as follows:

> "The APA authorizes suit by '[a] person suffering legal wrong because of agency action, or adversely affected or aggrieved by agency action within the meaning of a relevant statute.' 5 U.S.C. § 702. Where no other statute provides a private right of action, the 'agency action' complained of must be '*final* agency action.' § 704 (emphasis added). 'Agency action' is defined in § 551(13) to include 'the whole or a part of an agency rule, order, license, sanction, relief, or the equivalent or denial thereof, *or failure to act.*'(Emphasis added.) The APA provides relief for a failure to act in §706(1): 'The reviewing court shall . . . compel agency action unlawfully withheld or unreasonably delayed.'
>
> "Sections 702, 704, and 706(1) all insist upon an 'agency action,' either as the action complained of (in §§ 702 and 704) or as the action to be compelled (in § 706(1))."

Norton, 542 U.S. at 61–62. Thus, the Court held that in order to be viable, an APA claim seeking to compel an agency to act must point to "a *discrete* agency action that it is *required to take*." *Id.* at 64 (emphasis in original). This standard precludes "broad programmatic attack[s]." *Id.* The Court added:

> "The principal purpose of the APA limitations we have discussed—and of the traditional limitations upon mandamus from which they were derived—is to protect agencies from undue judicial interference with their lawful discretion, and to avoid judicial entanglement in abstract policy disagreements which courts lack both expertise and information to resolve."
>
> *Id.*

2. Discretion Is Not Unlimited

Page 3-43 – Replace the first full paragraph with the following:

In *Lincoln v. Vigil,* 508 U.S. 182 (1993), the Supreme Court concluded that, absent statutory elaboration, decisions about how to allocate funds within a lump-sum appropriation are committed to agency discretion by law. The Court noted that "the very point of a lump-sum appropriation is to give an agency the capacity to adapt to changing circumstances and meet its statutory responsibilities in what it sees as the most effective or desirable way." *Id.* at 191. Therefore, the Court held that judicial review of the agency's decision to discontinue a program that had been previously funded through a lump-sum appropriation was precluded. (See Chapter 6 for a more detailed discussion of the availability of appropriations.) *See also Hein v. Freedom From Religion Foundation, Inc.,* ___ U.S. ___, 127 S. Ct. 2553 (2007); 55 Comp. Gen. 307 (1975); B-278121, Nov. 7, 1997.

Page 3-43 – Replace the second full paragraph with the following:

Discretion must be exercised before the obligation is incurred. Approval after the fact is merely a condoning of what has already been done and does not constitute the exercise of discretion. 22 Comp. Gen. 1083 (1943); 14 Comp. Gen. 698 (1935); A-57964, Jan. 30, 1935. (This point should not be confused with an agency's occasional ability to ratify an otherwise unauthorized act. *See, e.g.,* B-306353, Oct. 26, 2005.)

Chapter 4

Availability of Appropriations: Purpose

Page 4-3 –		*Replace part of the index for section 11 as follows:*
11. Lobbying, Publicity or Propaganda, and Related Matters		
a.	Introduction	
b.	Penal Statutes	
c.	Appropriation Act Restrictions	
	(1)	Origin and general considerations
	(2)	Self-aggrandizement
	(3)	Covert propaganda
	(4)	Purely partisan materials
	(5)	Pending legislation: Overview
	(6)	Cases involving "grassroots" lobbying violations
	(7)	Pending legislation: Cases in which no violation was found
	(8)	Pending legislation: Providing assistance to private lobbying groups
	(9)	Promotion of legislative proposals: Prohibited activity short of grass roots lobbying...
	(10)Federal employees' communications with Congress	

A. General Principles

1. Introduction: 31 U.S.C. § 1301(a)

Page 4-6 – Replace the fourth paragraph with the following:

Simple, concise, and direct, this statute was originally enacted in 1809 (ch. 28, § 1, 2 Stat. 535, (Mar. 3, 1809)) and is one of the cornerstones of congressional control over the federal purse. Because money cannot be paid from the Treasury except under an appropriation (U.S. Const. art. I, § 9, cl. 7), and because an appropriation must be derived from an act of Congress, it is for Congress to determine the purposes for which an appropriation may be used. Simply stated, 31 U.S.C. § 1301(a) says that public funds may be used only for the purpose or purposes for which they were appropriated. It prohibits charging authorized items to the wrong appropriation, and unauthorized items to any appropriation. *See, e.g.,* B-302973, Oct. 6, 2004 (agency could not charge authorized activities such as cost comparison studies to an appropriation that specifically prohibits its use for such studies). Anything less would render congressional control largely meaningless. An earlier Treasury Comptroller was of the opinion that the statute did not make any new law, but merely codified what was already required under the Appropriations Clause of the Constitution. 4 Lawrence, First Comp. Dec. 137, 142 (1883).

2. Determining Authorized Purposes

Page 4-11 – Replace the first full paragraph with the following:

Once the purposes have been determined by examining the various pieces of legislation, 31 U.S.C. § 1301(a) comes into play to restrict the use of the appropriation to these purposes only, together with one final generic category of payments—payments authorized under general legislation applicable to all or a defined group of agencies and not requiring specific appropriations. For example, legislation enacted in 1982 amended 12 U.S.C. § 1770 to authorize federal agencies to provide various services, including telephone service, to employee credit unions. Pub. L. No. 97-320, § 515, 96 Stat. 1469, 1530 (Oct. 15, 1982). Prior to this legislation, an agency would have violated 31 U.S.C. § 1301(a) by providing telephone service to a credit union, even on a reimbursable basis, because this was not an authorized purpose under any agency appropriation. 60 Comp. Gen. 653 (1981). The 1982 amendment made the providing of special services to credit unions an authorized agency function, and hence an authorized purpose, which it could fund from unrestricted general operating appropriations. 66 Comp. Gen. 356 (1987). Similarly, a recently enacted statute gives agencies the discretion to use appropriated funds to pay the expenses their employees incur for obtaining professional credentials. 5 U.S.C. § 5757(a); B-289219, Oct. 29, 2002. *See also* B-302548, Aug. 20, 2004 (section 5757(a) does not authorize the agency to pay for an employee's membership in a professional association unless membership is a prerequisite to obtaining the professional license or certification). Prior to this legislation, agencies could not use appropriated funds to pay fees incurred by their employees in obtaining professional credentials. *See, e.g.,* 47 Comp. Gen. 116 (1967). Other examples are interest payments under the Prompt Payment Act (31 U.S.C. §§ 3901–3907) and administrative settlements less than $2,500 under the Federal Tort Claims Act (28 U.S.C. §§ 2671–2680).

Page 4-11 – Replace the second full paragraph with the following:

Where an appropriation specifies the purpose for which the funds are to be used, 31 U.S.C. § 1301(a) applies in its purest form to restrict the use of the funds to the specified purpose. For example, an appropriation for topographical surveys in the United States was not available for topographical surveys in Puerto Rico. 5 Comp. Dec. 493 (1899). Similarly, an appropriation to install an electrical generating plant in the customhouse building in Baltimore could not be used to install the plant in a nearby post office building, even though the plant would serve both buildings and thereby reduce operating expenses. 11 Comp. Dec. 724 (1905). An appropriation for the extension and remodeling of the State Department building was not available to construct a pneumatic tube delivery system between the State Department and the White House. 42 Comp. Gen. 226 (1962). In another example involving a line-item appropriation for a grant project, because the funds were made available for a specific grantee in a specific amount to accomplish a specific purpose, the agency could not grant less than Congress has directed by using some of the appropriation to pay its administrative costs. 72 Comp. Gen. 317 (1993); 69 Comp Gen. 660, 662 (1990). An appropriation to the Department of Labor for payment to the New York Workers' Compensation Board for the processing of claims related to the September 11, 2001, terrorist attack on the World Trade Center was not available to make payments to other New York State entities. B-303927, June 7, 2005. And, as noted previously, an appropriation for the "replacement" of state roads could not be used to make improvements on them. 41 Comp. Gen. 255 (1961).

Page 4-12 – Replace the first full paragraph with the following:

It is well settled, but warrants repeating, that even an expenditure that may be reasonably related to a general appropriation may not be paid out of that appropriation where the expenditure falls specifically within the scope of another appropriation. 63 Comp. Gen. 422 (1984); B-300325, Dec. 13, 2002; B-290005, July 1, 2002. It is also well settled that when two appropriations are available for the same purpose, the agency must select which to use, and that once it has made an election, the agency must continue to use the same appropriation for that purpose unless the agency, at the beginning of the fiscal year, informs Congress of its intent to change for the next fiscal year. B-307382, Sept. 5, 2006; B-272191, Nov. 4, 1997. *See also* 68 Comp. Gen. 337 (1989); 59 Comp. Gen. 518 (1980). An exception to this requirement is when Congress specifically authorizes the use of two appropriation accounts. B-272191, Nov. 4, 1997 (statutory language makes clear that Congress intended that the "funds appropriated to the Secretary [of the Army] for operation and maintenance" in the fiscal year 1993 Defense Appropriations Act are "[i]n addition to . . . the funds specifically appropriated for real property maintenance under the heading [RPM,D]" in that appropriation act).

3. New or Additional Duties

Page 4-16 – Replace the first full paragraph with the following:

Similarly, the Bureau of Land Management could use current appropriations to determine fair market value and to initiate negotiations with owners in connection with the acquisition of mineral interests under the Cranberry Wilderness Act,[9] even though actual acquisitions could not be made until funding was provided in appropriation acts. B-211306, June 6, 1983. *See also* B-290011, Mar. 25, 2002; B-211306,. June 6, 1983; B-153694, Oct. 23, 1964. Of course, an appropriation is not available if Congress has prohibited the agency from using it. In B-308715, Apr. 20, 2007, the Department of Energy is specifically barred under 42 U.S.C. § 7278 from using funds made available under an Energy and Water Development Appropriations Act to implement or finance any authorized loan guarantee program unless specific provision has been made for that program in an appropriations act. Since no provision was made, Energy could not use the Energy and Water appropriation to begin implementing the loan guarantee program.

B. THE "NECESSARY EXPENSE" DOCTRINE

1. The Theory

Page 4-21 – Replace the third paragraph with the following:

In addition to recognizing the differences among agencies when applying the necessary expense rule, we act to maintain a vigorous body of case law responsive to the changing needs of government. In this regard, our decisions indicate a willingness to consider changes in societal expectations regarding what constitutes a necessary expense. This flexibility is evident, for example, in our analysis of whether an expenditure constitutes a personal or an official expense. As will be discussed more fully later in the chapter, use of appropriations for such an expenditure is determined by continually weighing the benefit to the agency, such as the productivity, safety, recruitment, and retention of a dynamic workforce and other considerations enabling efficient, effective, and responsible government. We recognize, however, that these factors can change over time. B-302993, June 25, 2004 (modifying earlier decisions to reflect determination that purchase of kitchen appliances for use by agency employees in an agency facility is reasonably related to the efficient performance of agency activities, provides other benefits such as assurance of a safe workplace, and primarily benefits the agency, even though employees enjoy a collateral benefit); B-286026, June 12, 2001(overruling GAO's earlier decisions based on reassessment of the training opportunities afforded by examination review courses);. B-280759, Nov. 5, 1998 (overruling GAO's earlier decisions on the purchase of business cards). *See also* 71 Comp. Gen. 527 (1992) (eldercare is not a typical employee benefit provided to the nonfederal workforce and not one that the federal workforce should expect); B-288266, Jan. 27, 2003 (GAO explained it remained "willing to reexamine our case law" regarding light refreshments if it is shown to frustrate efficient, effective, and responsible government).

Page 4-22 – Replace the citations after the numbered paragraph 3 with the following:

E.g., B-303170, Apr. 22, 2005; 63 Comp. Gen. 422, 427–28 (1984); B-240365.2, Mar. 14, 1996; B-230304, Mar. 18, 1988.

Page 4-23 – Insert the following after the second full paragraph:

For example, in August 2004, in response to an elevated national security threat level with respect to Washington, D.C., the Capitol Police established the Security Traffic Checkpoint Program (STCP), which consisted of 14 security traffic checkpoints intended to secure all streets to the two main avenues leading to the Capitol building. Under this program, Capitol Police officers were required to staff the 14 checkpoints on a 24-hour, 7-days-a-week basis, with each officer working 12-hour shifts. During the STCP's operation from August 2, 2004, until November 23, 2004, the Capitol Police incurred approximately $1.3 to $1.5 million in overtime expenses every pay period. The Capitol Police financed the overtime expenses related to the program with money transferred to it from the Emergency Response Fund (ERF) established by Congress to, among other things, fund counterterrorism measures and support national security. Pub. L. No. 107-38, 115 Stat. 220 (Sept. 18, 2001). GAO was asked whether the use of the ERF for the STCP overtime payments was a proper use of the ERF appropriation. In finding that there was a reasonable nexus between the overtime expenditure and ERF appropriation charged, GAO stated:

> "Law enforcement agencies are entitled to discretion in deciding how best to protect our national institutions, such as the United States Congress, its Members, staff, and facilities. Here, the Capitol Police implemented the STCP in reaction to the heightened terror alert in August 2004 due to intelligence information suggesting the strong possibility of a terrorist attack at the Capitol Complex . . . The STCP checkpoints, clearly, were a counterterrorism measure, and certainly fall within the very broad scope of 'supporting national security.' . . . So long as the agency's use of the appropriation serves one of the . . . purposes for which the appropriation was enacted, the agency cannot be said to have used the appropriation improperly."

B-303964, Feb. 3, 2005, at 5.

Page 4-25 – Insert the following after the third paragraph:

Conference-related expenses may also be authorized as necessary expenses where the agency is authorized to host the conference. B-300826, Mar. 3, 2005. *Cf.* B-306424, Mar. 24, 2006 (Congress authorized the Presidio Trust to lease Presidio property as a venue for public and private events; thus the Trust's appropriations were available to cover expenses, such as the costs of providing audio equipment and related services, incurred during the National Academy of Public Administration's use of the Presidio's facilities for its 2005 annual Board of Directors meeting.)

Page 4-26 – Replace the first full paragraph with the following:

However, specific statutory authority is not essential. If participation is directly connected with and is in furtherance of the purposes for which a particular appropriation has been made, and an appropriate administrative determination is made to that effect, the appropriation is available for the expenditure. B-290900, Mar. 18, 2003 (Bureau of Land Management (BLM) may use its appropriated funds to pay its share of the cost to produce a brochure that educates the public regarding lighthouse preservation because the brochure supports BLM in meeting its responsibility under its lighthouse preservation program); B-286457, Jan. 29, 2001 (demolition of old air traffic control tower that would obstruct the view from the new one is directly connected with and in furtherance of the construction of a new tower such that the demolition expenses are covered by Federal Aviation Administration's appropriation act for tower construction); B-280440, Feb.

26, 1999 (Immigration and Naturalization Service's (INS) Salaries and Expenses appropriation is available to purchase medals to be worn by uniformed employees of the Border Patrol division of INS to commemorate the division's 75th anniversary). *See also* 16 Comp. Gen. 53 (1936); 10 Comp. Gen. 282 (1930); 7 Comp. Gen. 357 (1927); 4 Comp. Gen. 457 (1924).[15] Authority to disseminate information will generally provide adequate justification. *E.g.,* 7 Comp. Gen. 357; 4 Comp. Gen. 457. In addition, an agency may use appropriated funds to provide prizes or incentives to individuals to further the collection of information necessary to accomplish the agency's statutory mandate.[16] *See, e.g.,* B-304718, Nov. 9, 2005; 70 Comp. Gen. 720 (1991); B-286536, Nov. 17, 2000; B-230062, Dec. 22, 1988.

Page 4-29 – Insert the following after the third full paragraph:

Also, the Army could not use its Other Procurement, Army appropriation to pay contractors for logistical planning and plan implementation services related to the medical equipment items acquired using that appropriation because such services are not procurement activities and the Army's Operation and Maintenance appropriation was available and should be charged for such services. B-303170, Apr. 22, 2005.

2. General Operating Expenses

Page 4-34 – Replace the third full paragraph with the following:

The Salaries and Expenses appropriation of the Internal Revenue Service (IRS) could be used to procure credit bureau reports if administratively determined to be necessary in connection with investigating applicants for employment with the IRS. B-117975, Dec. 29, 1953. However, the Customs and Border Protection's (CBP) Salaries and Expenses appropriation was not available to pay for credit monitoring services for its employees in the New Orleans area who, as a result of Hurricane Katrina, were victims of identity theft. Neither government action nor inaction compromised the employees' identities, and in this case the CBP employees individually, not the government, would be the primary beneficiaries of the proposed credit monitoring, which was considered part of the employees' overall management of their personal finances. B-309604, Oct. 10, 2007.

Page 4-34 – Replace the fifth full paragraph with the following:

Outplacement assistance to employees may be regarded as a legitimate matter of agency personnel administration if the expenditures are found to benefit the agency and are reasonable in amount. 68 Comp. Gen. 127 (1988);

B-272040, Oct. 29, 1997. The Government Employees Training Act authorizes training in preparation for placement in another federal agency under conditions specified in the statute. 5 U.S.C. § 4103(b). Similarly, employee retirement education and retirement counseling, including individual financial planning for retirement, fall within the legitimate range of an agency's discretion to administer its personnel system and therefore are legitimate agency expenses. B-301721, Jan. 16, 2004.

C. SPECIFIC PURPOSE AUTHORITIES AND LIMITATIONS

5. Entertainment – Recreation – Morale and Welfare

Page 4-104 – Replace the first full paragraph with the following:

While feeding employees may not be regarded as a "necessary expense" as a general proposition, it may qualify when the agency is carrying out some particular statutory function where the necessity relationship can be established. Thus, in B-300826, Mar. 3, 2005, the National Institutes of Health (NIH) could use appropriated funds to provide meals and light refreshments to federal government (as well as nonfederal) attendees and presenters at an NIH-sponsored conference to coordinate and discuss Parkinson's disease research efforts within the scientific community. The conference was held in furtherance of NIH's statutory mission in 42 U.S.C. § 281 to "conduct and support" research with respect to particular diseases, and it was therefore within NIH's authority to pay for all legitimate, reasonable costs of hosting the formal conference. GAO determined that providing meals and refreshments was an allowable conference cost so long as the meals and refreshments were incidental to the conference, attendance at the meals was important to ensure full participation in the conference, and the meals and refreshments were part of a formal conference that included substantial functions occurring separately from when the food is served.

Other examples include B-201196, Mar. 4, 1982, in which GAO concluded that it was a permissible implementation of a statutory accident prevention program for the Marine Corps to set up rest stations on highways leading to a Marine base to serve coffee and doughnuts to Marines returning from certain holiday weekends. See also 65 Comp. Gen. 738 (1986) (refreshments at awards ceremonies), discussed later in this section. A related example is B-235163.11, Feb. 13, 1996, in which GAO determined that appropriated funds could be used to pay for the dinner of a nonfederal award recipient and her spouse at a National Science Foundation awards ceremony because of the statutory nature of the award. Exceptions of this type illustrate the relativity of the necessary expense doctrine pointed out earlier in our general discussion.

Page 4-119 – Replace the third paragraph with the following:

The purchase of equipment for use in other than an established cafeteria may also be authorized when the agency determines that the primary benefit of its use accrues to the agency by serving a valid operational purpose, such as providing for an efficient working environment or meeting health needs of employees, notwithstanding a collateral benefit to the employees. In B-302993, June 25, 2004, GAO approved the purchase of kitchen appliances, ordinarily considered to be personal in nature, for common use by employees in an agency facility. The appliances included refrigerators, microwaves, and commercial coffee makers. The agency demonstrated that equipping the workplace with these appliances was reasonably related to the efficient performance of agency activities and provided other benefits to the agency, including the assurance of a safe workplace. GAO also advised the agency that it should establish policies for uniform procurement and use of such equipment. In developing a policy, the agency should address the ongoing need for specific equipment throughout the building, the amount of the agency's appropriation budgeted for this purpose, price limitations placed on the equipment purchases, and whether the equipment should be purchased centrally or by individual units within headquarters. It is important that the policy ensure that appropriations are not used to provide any equipment for the sole use of an individual, and that the agency locate refrigerators, microwaves, and coffee makers acquired with appropriated funds only in common areas where they are available for use by all personnel. It should also be clear that appropriated funds will not be used to furnish goods, such as the coffee itself or microwaveable frozen foods, to be used in the kitchen area. These remain costs each employee is expected to bear.

The decision in B-302993, June 25, 2004, represented a departure from earlier cases which permitted such purchases under more restrictive circumstances where the agency could identify a specific need:

- B-173149, Aug. 10, 1971: purchase of a set of stainless steel cooking utensils for use by air traffic controllers to prepare food at a flight service station where there were no other readily accessible eating facilities and the employees were required to remain at their post of duty for a full 8-hour shift.

- B-180272, July 23, 1974: purchase of a sink and refrigerator to provide lunch facilities for the Occupational Safety and Health Review Commission where there was no government cafeteria on the premises.
- B-210433, Apr. 15, 1983: purchase of microwave oven by Navy facility to replace nonworking stove. Facility was in operation 7 days a week, some employees had to remain at their duty stations for 24-hour shifts, and there were no readily accessible eating facilities in the area during nights and weekends.
- B-276601, June 26, 1997: purchase of a refrigerator for personal food items of Central Intelligence Agency (CIA) employees. CIA headquarters facility was relatively distant from private eating establishments, the CIA did not permit delivery service to enter the facility due to security concerns, and the cafeteria served only breakfast and lunch.

Page 4-122 – Replace the first full paragraph with the following:

The decision at 60 Comp. Gen. 303 was expanded in B-199387, Mar. 23, 1982, to include small "samples" of ethnic foods prepared and served during a formal ethnic awareness program as part of the agency's equal employment opportunity program. In the particular program being considered, the attendees were to pay for their own lunches, with the ethnic food samples of minimal proportion provided as a separate event. Thus, the samples could be distinguished from meals or refreshments, which remain unauthorized. (The decision did not specify how many "samples" an individual might consume in order to develop a fuller appreciation.) Compare that situation to the facts in B-301184, Jan. 15, 2004, where GAO found that the U.S. Army Corps of Engineers' appropriation was not available to pay for the costs of food offered at the Corps' North Atlantic Division's February 2003 Black History Month program. The evidence in the record, including the time of the program, the food items served, and the amounts available, indicated that a meal, not a sampling of food, was offered.

Page 4-123 – Insert the following after the first full paragraph:

Similarly, GAO advised that serving refreshments purchased with appropriated funds to local children as part of the Forest Service's "Kid's Fishing Day" did not promote cultural awareness. While it may have been important that children learn to fish and appreciate the outdoors, such a goal did not advance federal EEO objectives. B-302745, July 19, 2004.

Page 4-125 – Insert the following, including the reference to new footnote number 72a, after the first paragraph:

An agency was found to have the requisite statutory authority to provide meals and refreshments to nonfederal personnel in B-300826, Mar. 3, 2005. In that case, GAO considered whether the National Institutes of Health (NIH) could use appropriated funds to provide meals and light refreshments to both federal and nonfederal attendees and presenters at a conference NIH was hosting on the latest scientific advances in treating Parkinson's disease. After reviewing NIH's statutory authority to conduct and support research to further the treatment of diseases, GAO concluded that NIH had the requisite authority to host the conference to which NIH had invited experts from the private sector as well as from other federal agencies, in addition to researchers from its own research institutes. NIH was not barred by the prohibition of 31 U.S.C. § 1345 from providing food to nonfederal personnel. As GAO explained, section 1345 has limited application, addressing only those conventions and other forms of assemblages or gatherings that private organizations seek to hold at government expense. B-300826, at 4 n.5. The decision cited 72 Comp. Gen. 229 (1993), which effectively overruled prior GAO decisions that applied section 1345 to meetings and conferences other than assemblages and gatherings that private organizations sought to hold at government expense. [72a] 72 Comp. Gen. at 231.

To determine whether the costs of meals and refreshments at such an agency-hosted conference are necessary to achieve the conference objectives, GAO established the following criteria: (1) the meals and refreshments are incidental to the formal conference, (2) attendance at the meals and when refreshments are served is important for the host agency to ensure attendees' full participation in essential discussion, lectures, or speeches concerning the purpose of the formal conference, and (3) the meals and refreshments are part of a formal conference that includes substantial functions occurring separately from when the food is served. Since the NIH proposal met these criteria, NIH could provide meals and refreshments at the Parkinson's disease conference. In so finding, GAO noted that the listed criteria must be applied on a case-by-case basis and advised federal agencies to develop procedures to ensure that the provision of meals and refreshments meet the criteria.

Another aspect of hosting a conference addressed in B-300826 concerned whether NIH could charge an attendance fee at the conference and retain the proceeds, or permit its contractor to do so. GAO held that without specific statutory authority an agency hosting a conference may not charge and retain an attendance fee, and the agency may not cure that lack of authority by engaging a contractor to do what it may not do. A contractor in this situation is "receiving money for the Government," and the miscellaneous receipts statute, 31 U.S.C. § 3302(b), requires that such funds must be deposited in the Treasury. This decision in B-300826 was affirmed in B-306663, Jan. 4, 2006. For more on the miscellaneous receipts statute, see Chapter 6, section E.2.

In 2006, Congress provided the Department of Defense (DOD) with specific authority to accept and retain fees from any individual or commercial participant in conferences, seminars, exhibitions, symposiums, or similar meetings conducted by DOD. Pub. L. No. 109-364, 120 Stat. 2083, 2395–96 (Oct. 17, 2006), *codified at* 10 U.S.C. § 2262. DOD may arrange for the collection of such fees either directly or through a contractor, and the fees may be collected in advance of the conference. 10 U.S.C. § 2262(a)(2). Amounts collected under this provision are credited to the appropriation or account from which the costs of the conference are paid, but any amount exceeding those costs must be deposited into the Treasury as miscellaneous receipts. 10 U.S.C. §§ 2262(b), (c). DOD is required to report annually on the number of conferences for which fees were collected, the amount of fees collected, and the actual costs of the conferences, including costs associated with any conference coordinators. 10 U.S.C. § 2262(d).

Page 4-125 – Insert the following as new footnote 72a:

[72a] The Department of Justice Office of Legal Counsel (OLC) has stated that it disagrees with our decision in B-300826, Mar. 3, 2005, insofar as it permits agencies to provide meals and light refreshments to nonfederal personnel. Memorandum Opinion for the General Counsel, Environmental Protection Agency, *Use of Appropriated Funds to Provide Light Refreshments to Non-Federal Participants at EPA Conferences,* OLC Opinion, Apr. 5, 2007.

Page 4-125 – Insert the following after the third paragraph:

The Veterans Benefits Administration (VBA) of the Department of Veterans Affairs (VA) inquired whether it may use appropriated funds to pay for incentives in the form of refreshments or light meals to increase participation in and the effectiveness of focus groups. Under 38 U.S.C. § 527(a), the VA is required to "measure and evaluate" its programs, and the VBA has been tasked with collecting this information. While VBA obtains information from a variety of sources, including mail or internet surveys and telephone interviews, VBA has determined that the use of focus groups is the best method of gathering this feedback and that the provision of refreshments to the participants is very helpful both in attracting these participants and getting useful information from the focus groups. Focus group participants are not VBA employees but are veterans and family members of veterans served by VBA. GAO concluded that, to the extent VBA determines that it needs to offer refreshments and light meals as an incentive to maximize participation by nonemployee veterans and their families in focus groups to fulfill its statutory requirement, VBA could use its appropriated funds to do so. However, GAO cautioned that VBA should provide such incentives pursuant to an appropriate, enforceable policy with procedures for approval to ensure that incentives are only provided when necessary and are used strictly for nonemployee focus groups. B-304718, Nov. 9, 2005.

7. Firefighting and Other Municipal Services

Page 4-154 – Insert the following after the first full paragraph:

In B-302230, Dec. 30, 2003, GAO found the District of Columbia's 9-1-1 emergency telephone system surcharge as originally enacted to be an impermissible tax on the federal government because the legal incidence of the tax fell on the federal government. Subsequently, the District of Columbia amended its law such that the legal incidence of the tax falls on the providers of telephone service, not the users of telephone service. Thus, federal agencies could pay bills that itemize the surcharge that the vendors must pay. *Id.*

8. Gifts and Awards

Page 4-155 – Replace the second full paragraph with the following:

An agency frequently wants to use gifts to attract attention to the agency or to specific programs. For example, gifts can be used as recruiting and retention tools, to commemorate an event, or to inform the public or agency employees about the agency. Appropriated funds may not be used for personal gifts, unless, of course, there is specific statutory authority.

B-307892, Oct. 11, 2006 (under 10 U.S.C. § 2261, Navy may use appropriated funds to purchase gifts for sailors to commemorate their reenlistment subject to regulations issued by the Secretary of Defense). *See also* 68 Comp. Gen. 226 (1989). To state the rule in this manner is to make it appear rather obvious. If, for example, a General Counsel decided it would be a nice gesture and improve employee morale to give each lawyer in the agency a Thanksgiving turkey, few would argue that the expense should be borne by the agency's appropriations. Appropriated funds could not be used because the appropriation was not made for this purpose (assuming, of course, that the agency has not received an appropriation for Thanksgiving turkeys) and because giving turkeys to lawyers is not reasonably necessary to carry out the mission at least of any agency that now exists. Most cases, however, are not quite this obvious or simple.

Page 4-166 – Replace the first full paragraph with the following:

The Incentive Awards Act applies to civilian agencies, civilian employees of the various armed services and specified legislative branch agencies. 5 U.S.C. § 4501. Within the judicial branch, it applies to the United States Sentencing Commission. *Id.*[103] While it does not apply to members of the armed forces, the Defense Department has very similar authority for military personnel in 10 U.S.C. § 1124.

Page 4-166 – Replace footnote number 103 with the following:

[103] The Sentencing Commission had not been covered prior to a 1988 amendment to the statute. *See* 66 Comp. Gen. 650 (1987). The Administrative Office of the United States Courts is no longer covered by the statute. Pub. L. No. 101-474, § 5(f), 104 Stat. 1100 (Oct. 30, 1990). The District of Columbia also is no longer covered. When the District of Columbia Home Rule Act was enacted into law, Pub. L. No. 93-198, 87 Stat. 777 (Dec. 24, 1973), the Act provided for the continuation of federal laws applicable to the District of Columbia government and its employees (that for the most part were in title 5 of the United States Code) until such time as the District enacted its own laws covering such matters. The District has adopted a number of laws exempting its employees from various provisions of title 5, and sections 4501 through 4506 are specifically superseded. *See* D.C. Official Code, 2001 ed. §1-632.02.

10. Insurance

Page 4-179 – Replace the first full paragraph with the following:

Another type of insurance which may not be paid for from appropriated funds is flight or accident insurance for employees on official travel. If a federal employee traveling by air on official business wishes to buy flight insurance, it is considered a personal expense and not reimbursable. B-309715, Sept. 25, 2007; 47 Comp. Gen. 319 (1967); 40 Comp. Gen. 11 (1960). Similarly nonreimbursable is trip cancellation insurance. 58 Comp. Gen. 710 (1979).

11. Lobbying and Related Matters

Page 4-188 – Replace the title of section 11 with the following:

11. Lobbying, Publicity or Propaganda, and Related Matters

Page 4-189 – Insert the following after the first full paragraph:

In addition to restrictions on lobbying, this section will explore restrictions on publicity or propaganda. Since 1951, appropriation acts have included provisions precluding the use of the appropriations for "publicity or propaganda." While Congress has never defined the meaning of publicity or propaganda, GAO has recognized three types of activities that violate the publicity or propaganda prohibitions: self-aggrandizement, covert propaganda, and materials that are purely partisan in nature.

Page 4-196 – Insert the following as the first paragraph under "(1) Origin and general considerations":

In addition to penal statutes imposing restrictions on lobbying, lobbying restrictions are found in appropriations acts. Restrictions on publicity or propaganda are found only in appropriations acts.

Page 4-197 – Replace the first paragraph and quotation with the following:

The publicity or propaganda prohibition made its first appearance in 1951. Members of Congress expressed concern over a speaking campaign promoting a national healthcare plan undertaken in the early 1950s by Oscar R. Ewing, the Administrator of the Federal Security Agency, a predecessor to the Department of Health and Human Services and the Social Security Administration. In reaction to this activity, Representative Lawrence R. Smith introduced the following provision, which was enacted in the Labor-Federal Security appropriation for 1952, Pub. L. No. 134, ch. 373, § 702, 65 Stat. 209, 223 (Aug. 31, 1951): "No part of any appropriation contained in this Act shall be used for publicity or propaganda purposes not heretofore authorized by the Congress." Later versions of this provision prohibit activity throughout the government: "No part of any appropriation contained *in this or any other Act* shall be used for publicity or propaganda purposes within the United States not heretofor authorized by the Congress."[117]

Page 4-197 – Replace footnote number 117 with the following:

[117] *See, e.g.*, the Transportation, Treasury, and related agencies' appropriations for 2005, Pub. L. No. 108-447, div. H, title VI, § 624, 118 Stat. 2809, 3278 (Dec. 8, 2004) (emphasis added).

Page 4-198 – Insert the following after the quotation and before the second full paragraph:

Although the publicity and propaganda prohibition has appeared in some form in the annual appropriations acts since 1951, the prohibitions themselves provide little definitional guidance as to what specific activities are publicity or propaganda. GAO has identified three activities that are prohibited by the publicity or propaganda prohibition—self-aggrandizement, covert propaganda, and purely partisan materials.

Page 4-198 – Replace the second full paragraph with the following:

In evaluating whether a given action violates a publicity or propaganda provision, GAO will rely heavily on the agency's administrative justification. In other words, the agency gets the benefit of any legitimate doubt. GAO will not accept the agency's justification where it is clear that the action falls into one of these categories. Before discussing these categories, two threshold issues must be noted.

Page 4-199 – Replace the first three paragraphs under "(2) Self-aggrandizement" and move the heading as follows:

As noted above, the broadest form of the publicity and propaganda restriction prohibits the use of appropriated funds "for publicity or propaganda purposes not authorized by Congress." A fiscal year 2005 governmentwide variation limits these restrictions to activities "within the United States."[121]

(2) Self-Aggrandizement

The Comptroller General first had occasion to construe this provision in 31 Comp. Gen. 311 (1952). The National Labor Relations Board asked whether the activities of its Division of Information amounted to a violation. Reviewing the statute's scant legislative history, the Comptroller General concluded that it was intended "to prevent publicity of a nature tending to emphasize the importance of the agency or activity in question." *Id.* at 313. Therefore, the prohibition would not apply to the "dissemination to the general public, or to particular inquirers, of information reasonably necessary to the proper administration of the laws" for which an agency is responsible. *Id.* at 314. Based on this interpretation, GAO concluded that the activities of the Board's Division of Information were not improper. The only thing GAO found that might be questionable, the decision noted, were certain press releases reporting speeches of members of the Board.

Thus, 31 Comp. Gen. 311 established the important proposition that the statute does not prohibit an agency's legitimate informational activities.

See also B-302992, Sept. 10, 2004; B-302504, Mar. 10, 2004;

B-284226.2, Aug. 17, 2000; B-223098.2, Oct. 10, 1986. It also established that the publicity or propaganda restriction prohibits "publicity of a nature tending to emphasize the importance of the agency or activity in question." 31 Comp. Gen. at 313. *See also* B-302504, Mar. 10, 2004; B-212069, Oct. 6, 1983. Such activity has become known as "self-aggrandizement."

Page 4-199 – Replace footnote number 121 with the following:

[121] Pub. L. No. 108-447, div. H, title VI, § 624, 118 Stat. 2809, 3278 (Dec. 8, 2004).

Page 4-200 – Replace the first full paragraph with the following:

In B-302504, Mar. 10, 2004, GAO considered a flyer and television and print advertisements that the Department of Health and Human Services (HHS) produced and distributed to inform Medicare beneficiaries of recently enacted changes to the Medicare program. While the materials had notable factual omissions and other weaknesses, GAO concluded that the materials were not self-aggrandizement because they did not attribute the enactment of new Medicare benefits to HHS or any of its agencies or officials.

There was also no violation found in B-303495, Jan. 4, 2005. In this case, the Office of National Drug Control Policy used the term "Drug Czar" to describe its director in video news releases it issued under the Drug-Free Media Campaign Act of 1998. The term had common, widespread, and long-standing usage by the media and members of Congress, and was not being used by the agency to persuade the public of the importance of the director. Rather, it was used as "nothing more than a sobriquet." *Id.*

Page 4-200 – Replace the third full paragraph with the following:

Other cases, in which GAO specifically found no self-aggrandizement, are B-284226.2, Aug. 17, 2000 (Department of Housing and Urban Development report and accompanying letter providing information to agency constituents about the impact of program reductions being proposed in Congress); B-212069, Oct. 6, 1983 (press release by Director of Office of Personnel Management excoriating certain Members of Congress who wanted to delay a civil service measure the administration supported); and B-161686, June 30, 1967 (State Department publications on Vietnam War). In none of these cases were the documents designed to glorify the issuing agency or official.

Page 4-202 – Replace the first paragraph under the heading "(3) Covert propaganda" with the following:

Another type of activity that GAO has construed as prohibited by the "publicity or propaganda not authorized by Congress" statute is "covert propaganda," defined as "materials such as editorials or other articles prepared by an agency or its contractors at the behest of the agency and circulated as the ostensible position of parties outside the agency." B-229257, June 10, 1988. A critical element of the violation is concealment from the target audience of the agency's role in sponsoring the material.

Id.; B-305368, Sept. 30, 2005; B-304228, Sept. 30, 2005; B-303495, Jan. 4, 2005; B-302710, May 19, 2004; B-306349, Sept. 30, 2005 (nondecision letter).

Page 4-202 – Insert the following after the second full paragraph:

In B-302710, May 19, 2004, GAO found that the Department of Health and Human Services (HHS) violated the prohibition when it produced and distributed prepackaged video news stories that did not identify the agency as the source of the news stories. Prepackaged news stories, ordinarily contained in video news releases, or "VNRs," have become a popular tool in the public relations industry. The prepackaged news stories may be accompanied by a suggested script, video clips known as "B-roll" film which news organizations can use either to augment their presentation of the prepackaged news story or to develop their own news reports in place of the prepackaged story, and various other promotional materials. These materials are produced in the same manner in which television news organizations produce materials for their own news segments, so they can be reproduced and presented as part of a newscast by the news organizations. The HHS news stories were part of a media campaign to inform Medicare recipients about new benefits available under the recently enacted Medicare Prescription Drug, Improvement, and Modernization Act of 2003. HHS designed its prepackaged video news stories to be indistinguishable from video segments produced by private news broadcasters, allowing broadcasters to incorporate them into their broadcasts without alteration. The suggested anchor lead-in scripts included in the package facilitated the unaltered use of the prepackaged news stories, announcing the package as a news story by fictional news reporters. HHS, however, did not include any statement in the news stories to advise the television viewing audience, the target of the purported news stories, that the agency wrote and produced the prepackaged news stories, and the television viewing audiences did not know that the stories they watched on television news programs *about the government* were, in fact, prepared *by the government*. *See also* B-304228, Sept. 30, 2005 (prepackaged news story produced by consultant hired by the Department of Education did not reveal to the target audience the

Department's role so it was covert propaganda in violation of the prohibition); B-303495, Jan. 4, 2005 (prepackaged news stories produced by the Office of National Drug Control Policy were covert propaganda in violation of the prohibition). *Cf.* B-307917, July 6, 2006 (newspaper article).

Page 4-202 – Replace the third full paragraph with the following:

A similar holding is 66 Comp. Gen. 707 (1987), involving newspaper articles and editorials in support of Central American policy. The materials were prepared by paid consultants at government request, and published as the work of nongovernmental parties. The decision also found that media visits by Nicaraguan opposition leaders, arranged by government officials but with that fact concealed, constituted another form of "covert propaganda." *See also* B-305368, Sept. 30, 2005 (Department of Education contract with radio and television personality to comment regularly on the No Child Left Behind Act without assuring that the Department's role was disclosed to the targeted audiences violated the publicity and propaganda prohibition);

B-129874, Sept. 11, 1978 ("canned editorials" and sample letters to the editor in support of Consumer Protection Agency legislation, had they been prepared, would have violated the law); B-306349, Sept. 30, 2005 (nondecision letter) (Department of Education urged to review newspaper article written by a Department of Education contractor which did not disclose the agency's involvement in its writing for possible publicity or propaganda violations). *Compare* B-304716, Sept. 30, 2005 (services provided by expert consultant hired by the Department of Health and Human Services, Administration for Children and Families (ACF), did not violate the publicity or propaganda prohibition since the one published article prepared by the consultant under the contract was published under the signature of the assistant secretary of ACF and the contract did not call for the consultant to write articles under her own name).

Page 4-202 – Insert the following after the last paragraph:

In B-302992, Sept. 10, 2004, the Forest Service produced video and print materials to explain and defend its controversial land and resource management plan for the Sierra Nevada Forest. Because the video and print materials clearly identified the Forest Service and the Department of Agriculture as the source of the materials, GAO concluded that they did not constitute covert propaganda. *See also* B-301022, Mar. 10, 2004 (the Office of National Drug Control Policy was clearly identified as the source of materials sent to members of the National District Attorneys Association concerning the debate over the legalization of marijuana).

In reaction to the growing use of prepackaged news stories within the government, GAO issued a circular letter to the heads of departments, agencies, and others concerned entitled *Prepackaged News Stories,* B-304272, Feb. 17, 2005. The letter fully explains the limitations imposed by the publicity or propaganda prohibition on the use of prepackaged news stories. It also explains when agencies are allowed to use prepackaged news stories, noting in particular that such use is valid so long as there is clear disclosure to the viewing audience that the material presented was prepared by or in cooperation with a government agency.

In May 2005, Congress enacted section 6076 of the Emergency Supplemental Appropriations Act for Defense, the Global War on Terror, and Tsunami Relief, 2005, Pub. L. No. 109-13, 110 Stat. 231, 301 (May 11, 2005). Section 6076 provided that no appropriations "may be used by an executive branch agency to produce any prepackaged news story intended for broadcast or distribution unless the story includes a clear notification within the text or audio of the prepackaged news story that the prepackaged news story was prepared or funded by that executive branch agency." *Id.* In the conference report submitted to both houses of Congress the conferees specifically noted GAO's analysis of covert propaganda and stated that section 6076 "*confirms* the opinion of the Government Accountability Office dated February 17, 2005 (B-304272)." H.R. Conf. Rep. No. 109-72, at 158–59 (2005) (emphasis added). The opinion to which the report was referring was the Comptroller General's circular letter which clearly stated that the critical element in determining whether prepackaged news stories constitute covert propaganda is whether the intended audience is informed of the source of the materials. B-304272, Feb. 17, 2005. Inasmuch as section 6076 "confirms" GAO's opinion, the section did not create new law or impose a new requirement. "Congress enacted section 6076 to emphasize that the publicity or propaganda prohibition always restricted the use of appropriations to disseminate information without proper source attribution." B-307917, July 6, 2006, at 2 (concerning newspaper article without source attribution that agency contracted for before passage of section 6076). Therefore, transactions entered into before the date of enactment of section 6076 are held to the same requirement for source attribution. *Id.*

(4) Purely Partisan Materials

A third category of materials identified in GAO case law as violating the publicity or propaganda prohibition is purely partisan materials. To be characterized as purely partisan in nature, the offending materials must be found to have been "designed to aid a political party or candidate." B-147578, Nov. 8, 1962. It is axiomatic that funds appropriated to carry out a particular program would not be available for political purposes. *See* B-147578, Nov. 8, 1962.

It is often difficult to determine whether materials are political or not because "the lines separating the nonpolitical from the political cannot be precisely drawn." *Id.*; B-144323, Nov. 4, 1960. *See also* B-130961, Oct. 16, 1972. An agency has a legitimate right to explain and defend its policies and respond to attacks on that policy. B-302504, Mar. 10, 2004. A standard GAO applies is that the use of appropriated funds is improper only if the activity is "completely devoid of any connection with official functions." B-147578, Nov. 8, 1962. As stated in B-144323, Nov. 4, 1960:

> "[The question is] whether in any particular case a speech or a release by a cabinet officer can be said to be so completely devoid of any connection with official functions or so political in nature that it is not in furtherance of the purpose for which Government funds were appropriated, thereby making the use of such funds ...unauthorized. This is extremely difficult to determine in most cases as the lines separating the nonpolitical from the political cannot be precisely drawn.
>
> "...As a practical matter, even if we were to conclude that the use of appropriated funds for any given speech or its release was unauthorized, the amount involved would be small, and difficult to ascertain; and the results of any corrective action might well be more technical than real."

While GAO has reviewed materials to determine whether they are partisan in nature, to date there are no opinions or decisions of the Comptroller General concluding that an agency's informational materials were so purely partisan as to constitute impermissible publicity or propaganda. In 2000, GAO concluded that an information campaign by the Department of Housing and Urban Development (HUD) using a widely disseminated publication, entitled *Losing Ground: The Impact of Proposed HUD Budget Cuts on America's Communities,* had not violated the prohibition. B-284226.2, Aug. 17, 2000. In the publication, HUD criticized what it called "deep cuts" in appropriations that were proposed by the House Appropriations Committee for particular HUD programs. The publications stated that, if enacted, the "cuts would have a devastating impact on families and communities nationwide." GAO found that this publication was a legitimate exercise of HUD's duty to inform the public of government policies, and that HUD had a right to justify its policies to the public and rebut attacks against those policies.

In B-302504, Mar. 10, 2004, GAO examined a flyer and print and television advertisements about changes to Medicare enacted by the Medicare Prescription Drug, Improvement, and Modernization Act of 2003, Pub. L. No. 108-173, 117 Stat. 2066 (Dec. 8, 2003). The flyer contained information about new prescription drug benefits and price discount cards. GAO noted that while the materials contained opinion and notable factual omissions, the materials did not constitute impermissible publicity or propaganda. GAO explained:

> "To restrict all materials that have some political content or express support of an Administration's policies would significantly curtail the recognized and legitimate exercise of the Administration's authority to inform the public of its policies, to justify its policies and to rebut attacks on its policies. It is important for the public to understand the philosophical underpinnings of the policies advanced by elected officials and their staff in order for the public to evaluate and form opinions on those policies."
>
> *Id.* at 10.

In B-302992, Sept. 10, 2004, GAO upheld the Forest Service's right to produce and distribute a brochure and video materials regarding its controversial policy on managing wildfire in the Sierra Nevada Forest. Because the materials sought to explain hundreds of pages of scientific data, official opinions, and documents of the Forest Service, they were not comprehensive and did not explain all the positive and negative aspects of the thinning policies adopted in its regional forest plan. GAO concluded that the Forest Service had the authority to disseminate information about its programs and policies and to defend those policies.

Apart from considerations of whether any particular law has been violated, GAO has taken the position in two audit reports that the government should not disseminate misleading information. In 1976, the former Energy Research and Development Administration (ERDA) published a pamphlet entitled *Shedding Light On Facts About Nuclear Energy*. Ostensibly created as part of an employee motivational program, ERDA printed copies of the pamphlet far in excess of any legitimate program needs, and inundated the state of California with them in the months preceding a nuclear safeguards initiative vote in that state. While the pamphlet had a strong pro-nuclear bias and urged the reader to "Let your voice be heard," the pamphlet did not violate any anti-lobbying statute because applicable restrictions did not extend to lobbying at the state level. B-130961-O.M., Sept. 10, 1976. However, GAO's review of the pamphlet found it to be oversimplified and misleading. GAO characterized it as propaganda not suitable for distribution to anyone, employees or otherwise, and recommended that ERDA cease further distribution and recover and destroy any undistributed copies. *See* GAO, *Evaluation Of the Publication and Distribution Of "Shedding Light On Facts About Nuclear Energy,"* EMD-76-12 (Washington, D.C.: Sept. 30, 1976).

In a later report, GAO reviewed a number of publications related to the Clinch River Breeder Reactor Project, a cooperative government/industry demonstration project, and found several of them to be oversimplified and distorted propaganda, and as such questionable for distribution to the public. However, the publications were produced by the private sector components of the Project and paid for with utility industry contributions and not with federal funds. GAO recommended that the Department of Energy work with the private sector components in an effort to eliminate this kind of material, or at the very least ensure that such publications include a prominently displayed disclaimer statement making it clear that the material was not government approved. GAO, *Problems With Publications Related To The Clinch River Breeder Reactor Project,* EMD-77-74 (Washington, D.C.: Jan. 6, 1978).

Page 4-203 – Renumber section (4) as follows:
(5) Pending legislation: Overview
Page 4-207 – Renumber section (5) as follows:
(6) Cases involving "grassroots" lobbying violations
Page 4-210 – Renumber section (6) as follows:
(7) Pending legislation: Cases in which no violation was found

Page 4-212 – Insert the following after the first paragraph:

In another case, the Social Security Administration (SSA), in its annual mailing of employment benefit reports to American workers, included material concerning the Social Security system's potential financial problems and legislative initiatives to reform the Social Security program. Since none of the material called on the public to contact Congress and urge it to support SSA's position on this or any other matter, GAO determined that there was no violation of the grassroots lobbying prohibition. GAO rejected the suggestion that the standard ought to be an assessment of the agency's intent and whether the agency's message *would be likely* to influence the public to contact Congress. The standard requiring evidence of a clear appeal by the agency to the public to contact congressional members to urge them to support the agency's position is based upon the language and legislative history of the grassroots lobbying provisions. Moreover, the standard is consistent with a proper respect for the right and responsibility of federal agencies to communicate with the public and Congress regarding policies and activities. GAO stated:

> "We have no reason to think that Congress meant to preclude government officials from saying anything that might possibly cause the public to think about or take positions on the issues of the day and, as a result, contact their elected representatives. To the contrary, we see the free and open exchange of ideas and views as central to our political system and, accordingly, remain reluctant to construe these laws in such a way that would unnecessarily or excessively constrain agency communications with the public or Congress."
> B-304715, Apr. 27, 2005.

Page 4-213 – Renumber section (7) as follows:
(8) Pending legislation: Providing assistance to private lobbying groups

Page 4-215 – Renumber section (8) as follows:
(9) Promotion of legislative proposals: Prohibited activity short of grass roots lobbying

Pages 4-218 to 4-219 – Delete the entire section (9) entitled "Dissemination of political or misleading information"; the information contained therein has been integrated into the new section "(4) Purely partisan materials," above.

Page 4-219 – Insert the following after the third paragraph as a new section 11.c.(10):

(10) Federal employees' communications with Congress Since 1998, annual appropriations acts each year have contained a governmentwide prohibition on the use of appropriated funds to pay the salary of any federal official who prohibits or prevents another federal employee from communicating with Congress. *See* Pub. L. No. 105-61, § 640, 111 Stat. 1272, 1318 (Oct. 10, 1997). Specifically, this provision states:

> "No part of any appropriation contained in this or any other Act shall be available for the payment of the salary of any officer or employee of the Federal Government, who . . . prohibits or prevents, or

> attempts or threatens to prohibit or prevent, any other officer or employee of the Federal Government from having any direct oral or written communication or contact with any Member, committee, or subcommittee of the Congress in connection with any matter pertaining to the employment of such other officer or employee or pertaining to the department or agency of such other officer or employee in any way, irrespective of whether such communication or contact is at the initiative of such other officer or employee or in response to the request or inquiry of such Member, committee, or subcommittee."

Pub. L. No. 108-199, div. F, title VI, § 618, 188 Stat. 3, 354 (Jan. 23, 2004); Pub. L. No. 108-7, div. J, title VI, § 620, 117 Stat. 11, 468 (Feb. 20, 2003). This provision has its antecedents in several older pieces of legislation, including section 6 of the Lloyd-La Follette Act of 1912, Pub. L. No. 336, ch. 389, 66 Stat. 539, 540 (Aug. 24, 1912), which stated: "The right of persons employed in the civil service of the United States, either individually or collectively, to petition Congress, or any Member thereof, or to furnish information to either House of Congress, or to any committee or member thereof, shall not be denied or interfered with."

Congress enacted section 6 in response to concern over executive orders by Presidents Theodore Roosevelt and Howard Taft that prohibited federal employees from contacting Congress except through the head of their agency. The legislative history of this provision indicates that Congress intended to advance two goals: to preserve the First Amendment rights of federal employees regarding their working conditions and to ensure that Congress had access to programmatic information from frontline federal employees. *See* H.R. Rep. No. 62-388, at 7 (1912); 48 Cong. Rec. 5634, 10673 (1912).

In B-302911, Sept. 7, 2004, GAO concluded that the Department of Health and Human Services violated this provision by paying the salary of the Director of the Centers for Medicare and Medicaid Services (CMS) who prohibited the CMS Chief Actuary from providing certain cost estimates of Medicare legislation to Congress. The Director specifically instructed the Chief Actuary not to respond to any requests for information and advised that there would be adverse consequences if he released any information to Congress. GAO recognized that certain applications of the provision could raise constitutional separation of powers concerns; however, there was no controlling judicial opinion declaring the provision unconstitutional. GAO found that the provision, as applied to the facts in this case, precluded the payment of the CMS Director's salary because he specifically prevented another employee from communicating with Congress, particularly in light of the narrow, technical nature of the information requested by Congress and Congress's need for the information in carrying out its constitutional legislative duties.

Page 4-221 – Replace footnote 139 with the following:

[139] Pub. L. No. 104-65, 109 Stat. 691 (Dec. 19, 1995). For a discussion of the constitutionality of the Byrd Amendment in the grant context after passage of Public Law 104-65, see *United States v. National Training and Information Center,* No. 06-C-7076 (N.D. Ill. Aug. 23, 2007).

Page 4-227 – Replace the third full paragraph with the following:

A 1983 decision illustrates another form of information dissemination that is permissible without the need for specific statutory support. Military chaplains are required to hold religious services for the commands to which they are assigned. 10 U.S.C. § 3547. Publicizing such information as the schedule of services and the names and telephone numbers of installation chaplains is an appropriate extension of this duty. Thus, GAO advised the Army that it could procure and distribute calendars on which this information was printed. 62 Comp. Gen. 566 (1983). Applying a similar rationale, the decision also held that information on the Community Services program, which provides various social services for military personnel and their families, could be included. *See also* B-301367, Oct. 23, 2003 (affixing decals of the major units assigned to an Air Force base onto a nearby utility company water tower to inform the public of military activity in the area is a permissible use of appropriated funds); B-290900, Mar. 18, 2003 (approving the Bureau of Land Management's use of appropriated funds to pay its share of the costs of disseminating information under a cooperative agreement); B-280440, Feb. 26, 1999 (allowing the Border Patrol's use of appropriated funds to purchase uniform medals that, in part, served to advance "knowledge and appreciation for the agency's history and mission").

Page 4-232 – Replace the first full paragraph with the following:

A statute originally enacted in 1913, now found at 5 U.S.C. § 3107, provides: "Appropriated funds may not be used to pay a publicity expert unless specifically appropriated for that purpose." This provision applies to all appropriated funds. GAO has consistently noted certain difficulties in enforcing the statute. In GAO's first substantive discussion of 5 U.S.C. § 3107, the Comptroller General stated "[i]n its present form, the statute is ineffective." A-61553, May 10, 1935. The early cases[151] identified three problem areas, summarized in B-181254(2), Feb. 28, 1975.

Page 4-233 – Insert the following after the second paragraph:

The legislative history of section 3107 provides some illumination. While it is not clear what was meant by "publicity expert," there are indications that the provision would prohibit the use of press agents "to extol or to advertise" the agency or individuals within the agency. *See, e.g.*, 50 Cong. Rec. 4410 (1913) (comments of Representative Fitzgerald, chairman of the committee that reported the bill)). There are also indications that the provision should not interfere with legitimate information dissemination regarding agency work or services. When some members expressed concern that the provision may affect the hiring of experts to "mak[e] our farm bulletins more readable to the public and more practical in their make-up," supporters indicated that such activities would not be restricted by passage of the provision. *Id.*. at 4410 (colloquy between Representatives Lever and Fitzgerald).

Page 4-234 – Insert the following after the first partial paragraph:

GAO revisited the statute in B-302992, Sept. 10, 2004. The Forest Service had hired a public relations firm to help produce and distribute materials regarding its controversial land and resource management plan in the Sierra Nevada Forest, a plan consisting of hundreds of pages of scientific data and opinions. The Forest Service had hired the public relations firm to help make the plan's scientific content more understandable to the public and media. GAO concluded that the Forest Service had not violated section 3107. GAO said that section 3107 was not intended to impede legitimate informational functions of agencies and does not prohibit agencies from paying press agents and public affairs officers to facilitate and manage dissemination of agency information. GAO stated: "Instead, what Congress intended to prohibit with section 3107 is paying an individual 'to extol or to advertise' the agency, an activity quite different from disseminating information to the citizenry about the agency, its policies, practices, and products." B-302992, Sept. 10, 2004.

In 2005, GAO considered whether the Social Security Administration's (SSA) use of the Gallup Organization to poll the public on Social Security program issues violated 5 U.S.C. § 3107. Citing to the discussion of the legislative history of section 3107 in B-302992, Sept. 10, 2004, GAO determined that SSA did not hire Gallup to—nor did Gallup in fact—extol or advertise SSA or individuals within SSA. Rather, SSA hired Gallup to engage in the legitimate agency activity of collecting information that the agency needed in order to carry out its Social Security program. SSA's authority to survey the general public on its knowledge of the Social Security program and programs financing is inherent in the agency's authority to administer that program, 42 U.S.C. § 901(b). Since Gallup was assisting SSA in this endeavor, Gallup was not a "publicity expert" within the meaning of section 3107. B-305349, Dec. 20, 2005.

12. Membership Fees

Page 4-234 – Replace the first full paragraph with the following and insert new footnote number 152a as follows:

Appropriated funds may not be used to pay membership fees of an employee of the United States in a society or association. 5 U.S.C. § 5946. The prohibition does not apply if an appropriation is expressly available for that purpose, or if the fee is authorized under the Government Employees Training Act. Under the Training Act, membership fees may be paid if the fee is a necessary cost directly related to the training or a condition precedent to undergoing the training. 5 U.S.C. § 4109(b).[152a]

Page 4-234 – Insert the following for new footnote number 152a:

[152a] The District of Columbia has specifically exempted its employees from the provisions of 5 U.S.C. § 5946 as well as the Government Employees Training Act, 5 U.S.C. ch. 41. *See* D.C. Official Code, 2001 ed. § 1-632.02.

Page 4-236 – Replace the first full paragraph with the following:

As noted, an agency may purchase membership in its own name in a society or association since 5 U.S.C. § 5946 prohibits only memberships for individual employees. The distinction, however, is not a distinction in name only. An expenditure for an agency membership must be justified on a "necessary expense" theory. To do this, the membership must provide benefits to the agency itself. For example, in 31 Comp. Gen. 398 (1952), the Economic Stabilization Agency was permitted to become a member of a credit association because members could purchase credit reports at reduced cost and the procurement of credit reports was determined to be necessary to the enforcement of the Defense Production Act. In 33 Comp. Gen. 126 (1953), the Office of Technical Services, Commerce Department, was permitted to purchase membership in the American Management Association. The appropriation involved was an appropriation under the Mutual Security Act to conduct programs including technical assistance to Europe, and the membership benefit to the agency was the procurement of Association publications for foreign trainees and foreign productivity centers. *See also* B-305095, Dec. 8, 2005 (the United States Chemical Safety and Hazard Investigation Board appropriation is available to pay the membership fee for the Board to become a corporate associate member of the Risk Management and Decision Processes Center of the Wharton School, University of Pennsylvania, since the Board has determined that such membership will assist the Board in carrying out its duties under 42 U.S.C. § 7412(r)(6)); 70 Comp. Gen. 190 (1991) (prohibition in 5 U.S.C. § 5946 does not prohibit an agency from using appropriated funds to purchase access for its employees to a private fitness center's exercise facilities as part of the agency's health service program as authorized by 5 U.S.C. § 7901); B-241706, June 19, 1991 (Public Health Service may reimburse physicians for annual medical staff dues since hospital privileges are essential to the performance of the agency's business); B-236763, Jan. 10, 1990 (GAO may pay fees for agency membership in certain professional organizations and designate appropriate GAO employees to attend functions for recruitment purposes).

Page 4-239 – Replace the second paragraph with the following:

Compare that case with the decision in B-286026, June 12, 2001, in which the Pension Benefit Guaranty Corporation (PBGC) asked whether it could use appropriated funds to pay, as training costs, fees for actuary accreditation. PBGC employs a number of actuaries to calculate pension benefits. Although actuaries do not need a professional license for employment, as part of a collective bargaining agreement PBGC proposed to use training funds to send actuaries to the examination review courses, provide on-the-job study time, and pay for the accreditation examinations. PBGC determined that this course of study and testing would enhance the ability of the PBGC actuaries to carry out their assignments. PBGC has the discretion under the Government Employees Training Act to determine that the review courses constitute appropriate training for its actuaries. Accordingly, GAO agreed that PBGC has authority, under 5 U.S.C. § 4109(a), to use appropriated funds for review courses and on-the-job study time. However, there was no authority to pay the cost of the accreditation examination itself, since a licensing accreditation examination does not fall within the Government Employees Training Act's definition of training. In the absence of statutory authority, an agency may not pay the costs of its employees taking licensing examinations since professional accreditation is personal to the employee and should be paid with personal funds. Here, the actuarial accreditation belongs to the employee personally and would remain so irrespective of whether the employee remains with the federal government.

The PBGC decision, B-286026, June 12, 2001, predated enactment of 5 U.S.C. § 5757, which gave agencies the discretionary authority to reimburse employees for expenses incurred in obtaining professional credentials, including the costs of examinations. In B-302548,. Aug. 20, 2004, GAO determined that under 5 U.S.C. § 5757, an agency may pay only the expenses required to obtain the license or official certification needed to practice a particular profession. In that case, an employee who was a certified public accountant (CPA) asked her agency to pay for her membership in the California Society of Certified Public Accountants, which is voluntary and not a prerequisite for obtaining a CPA license in California. GAO held that payment for voluntary memberships in organizations of already credentialed professionals is prohibited under 5 U.S.C. § 5946, and section 5757 does not provide any authority to pay such fees where the membership in the organization is not a prerequisite to obtaining the professional credential. Section 5757 is discussed in more detail in this chapter in the next section on attorneys' expenses related to admission to the bar, and in section C.13.e on professional qualification expenses.

Page 4-242 – Replace the first paragraph with the following:

In 2001, section 1112 of the National Defense Authorization Act for Fiscal Year 2002, Pub. L. No. 107-107, 115 Stat. 1238 (Dec. 28, 2001) amended title 5, United States Code, by adding a new section 5757. Under 5 U.S.C. § 5757(a), agencies may, at their discretion, use appropriated funds to pay expenses incurred by employees to obtain professional credentials, state-imposed and professional licenses, professional accreditations, and professional certifications, including the costs of examinations to obtain such credentials. This authority is not available to pay such fees for employees in or seeking to be hired into positions excepted from the competitive service because of the confidential, policy-determining, policymaking, or policy-advocating character of the position. 5 U.S.C. § 5757(b). Nothing in the statute or its legislative history defines or limits the terms "professional credentials," "professional accreditation," or "professional certification." Agencies have the discretion to determine whether resources permit payment of credentials, and what types of professional expenses will be paid under the statute. Thus, if an agency determines that the fees its attorneys must pay for admission to practice before federal courts are in the nature of professional credentials or certifications, the agency may exercise its discretion under 5 U.S.C. § 5757 and pay those fees out of appropriated funds. B-289219, Oct. 29, 2002.

Also, GAO has stated that under 5 U.S.C. § 5757 an agency may pay the expenses of employees' memberships in state bar associations when membership is required to maintain their licenses to practice law. *See* B-302548, Aug. 20, 2004 (note that this decision concerned membership in a certified public accountants' (CPA) professional organization that was not required as a condition of the CPA license).

Page 4-253 – Replace the third paragraph with the following:

Another related line of decisions addresses the purchase of bottled drinking water for use in federal work facilities where the safety of municipal or locally provided water is at issue. Generally, appropriated funds are not available to pay for bottled water for the personal use of employees. GAO has made an exception where a building's water supply is unhealthy or unpotable. See, for example, B-247871, Apr. 10, 1992, where a problem with the water supply system in a building caused lead content to exceed the maximum contaminant level and justified the purchase of bottled water for employees until the problems with the system could be resolved. *Compare* B-303920, Mar. 21, 2006 (relief denied to certifying officer who improperly approved payments for bottled water for employees where there was no evidence that drinking water in the building was unhealthy).

Page 4-259 – Insert the following before the last paragraph:

A different type of situation arose in B-307316, Sept. 7, 2006. An Army captain held dual citizenship with the United States and with Turkey. In order to obtain a security clearance required for his assignment to the United States Army Center for Health Promotion and Preventive Medicine (Army Center), he had to renounce his Turkish citizenship. GAO determined that the expenses incurred for the renunciation of Turkish citizenship in order to obtain the security clearance were primarily for the benefit of the government since the required security clearance provided assurance to the government that sensitive information will be safe and the renunciation facilitated the granting of the clearance. Any personal benefit the captain would receive from the renunciation was incidental to the performance of his duties. Therefore, the Army Center could reimburse the captain for the renunciation expenses.

Page 4-260 – Replace the first paragraph with the following:

Neither the statute nor its legislative history defines the terms "professional credentials," "professional accreditation," and "professional certification." The statute and the 1994 decision together appear to cover many, if not most, qualification expenses that GAO previously found to be personal to the employee, including actuarial accreditation (B-286026, June 12, 2001), licenses to practice medicine (B-277033, June 27, 1997), a Certified Government Financial Manager designation (B-260771, Oct. 11, 1995), and professional engineering certificates (B-248955, July 24, 1992). See also B-302548, Aug. 20, 2004 (certified public accountant fees) and section C.12.b of this chapter for a discussion of attorneys' bar membership fees.

Page 4-264 – Replace the last partial paragraph with the following:

In 56 Comp. Gen. 81 (1976), the rationale of these cases was extended to Armed Forces change of command ceremonies. The decision held that the cost of printing invitations to a change of command ceremony for a Coast

Guard vessel could be paid from the Coast Guard's appropriations for operating expenses. In view of the traditional role of change of command ceremonies in the military, the Comptroller General concluded that the invitations were not inherently personal. (The case was therefore distinguishable from the decisions previously discussed prohibiting the use of public funds for greeting cards.) In another case, the expenditure of official reception and representation (OR and R) funds for costs of a change of command reception were determined to be payable from OR and R funds because the reception met the prerequisites for an "official reception for an incoming commander." 69 Comp. Gen. 242 (1990). (See section C.5 of this chapter for a more general discussion of related subject matter.)

Page 4-272 – Insert the following, including the reference to new footnote number 166a, after the first partial paragraph:

As a general rule, then, employees must bear the costs of transportation between their residences and official duty locations, even when unusual conditions may increase commuting costs. 60 Comp. Gen. 633, 635 (1981). Congress has authorized agencies to use appropriations for "the maintenance, operation, or repair of any passenger carrier," but "only to the extent that such carrier is used to provide transportation for official purposes." 31 U.S.C. § 1344(a)(1). It has specified that "transporting any individual . . . between such individual's residence and such individual's place of employment is not transportation for an official purpose." *Id.*

For example, in B-305864, Jan. 5, 2006, GAO held that the United States Capitol Police (USCP) could not use appropriated funds for a shuttle bus service from its parking lot to a new USCP facility or any other USCP building, where the only purpose of the shuttle service is to facilitate the commutes of USCP employees. The employee's arrival at the parking lot is viewed as an intermediate stop—like a subway or bus stop—within the totality of the commute from home to office. Therefore, the trip from the parking lot to the new USCP facility is part of the employee's commute and a personal expense. GAO noted that there would be no objection to the use of appropriated funds for a shuttle bus from USCP headquarters to the new facility and other USCP buildings, so long as USCP established a legitimate operational need to shuttle persons among those buildings and its purpose is not to aid employees' commutes. If USCP established a legitimate operational need for shuttle service among USCP buildings, there would also be no objection to any incidental use of the service by USCP employees to complete their home-to-work commutes, provided, of course, that there is no additional expenditure of time or money by the government in order to accommodate these riders. *Id.*

Although generally agencies may not pay commuting costs, agencies may exercise administrative discretion and provide transportation on a temporary basis when there is a clear and present danger to government employees or an emergency threatens the performance of vital government functions. 62 Comp. Gen. 438, 445 (1983). Under 31 U.S.C. § 1344(b)(9), an agency may provide for home-to-work transportation for an employee if the agency head determines that "highly unusual circumstances present a clear and present danger, that an emergency exists, or that other compelling operational considerations make such transportation essential to the conduct of official business." Section 1344(b)(9) also stipulates, however, that exceptions granted under it must be "in accordance with" 31 U.S.C. § 1344(d), which limits emergency exceptions to periods of up to 15 calendar days, subject to periodic renewal for up to a total of 180 additional calendar days, under specified detailed procedures.[166a]

GAO had occasion to consider the provisions in 31 U.S.C. § 1344 in B-307918, Dec. 20, 2006. The National Logistic Support Center (NLSC) was created by the National Oceanic and Atmospheric Administration to maintain a stockpile warehouse and ship replacement parts and equipment crucial to ensuring the proper functioning of equipment in the weather forecasting stations across the country. Since NLSC receives between 200 and 400 requests each year for emergency service outside of normal office hours, NLSC schedules employees to attend to these emergency, after-hours service requests on an "on-call" basis. When NLSC receives a request for after-hours emergency service, it notifies the on-call employees who return from their homes to their NLSC offices to respond to the requests, prepare the required parts for shipment to the affected weather station, deliver them to the shipping vendor, and return home. GAO determined that the prohibition in 31 U.S.C. § 1344(a)(1) precluded NLSC from using appropriated funds to reimburse its employees for the mileage between their residences and their NLSC offices since the statute precludes the payment of commuting expenses regardless of whether it is incident to a regular work schedule or the on-call work schedule described here. The emergency exception recognized in 31 U.S.C. §§ 1344(b)(9) and (d) did not apply because it is limited to brief, specific periods and NLSC's proposal contemplated reimbursing the on-call employees for commuting costs on a continual basis—without limit or end date.

Page 4-272 – Insert the following text for new footnote number 166a:

[166a] The detailed procedures require agencies to make written determinations that name the specific employees, explain the reasons for their exemption, and specify the duration of their exemptions; they preclude

agency heads from delegating this authority to another; and they require congressional notification of the above information for each exemption granted. 31 U.S.C. § 1344(d). Other subsections require the General Services Administration to promulgate governmentwide regulations and require agencies to maintain logs detailing all home-to-work transportation provided by the agency. 31 U.S.C. §§ 1344(e), 1344(f).

Page 4-274 – Insert the following after the first partial paragraph:

In 2007, GAO considered whether an agency may use its appropriated funds to reimburse employees for home high-speed internet access under its telecommuting program. Public Law 104-52 requires that the agency ensure that adequate safeguards against private misuse exist and that the service is necessary for direct support of the agency's mission. Pub. L. No. 104-52, § 620. As part of its program, the Patent and Trademark Office (PTO) would require telecommuting employees to maintain high speed internet access that meets certain minimum technical requirements at their residence or other designated alternative work site, and it proposed to reimburse participating employees for the costs incurred in their use of the internet access related to PTO work. Employees would be eligible for 50 or 100 percent reimbursement (up to a maximum of $100 per month) depending on the amount of monthly business use of the internet service. To obtain reimbursement, employees each month would be required to submit copies of invoices from the internet service provider and to attest to the appropriate percentage of internet service used for work-related purposes. GAO determined that PTO could use its appropriated funds to reimburse telecommuting employees for the costs of the high-speed internet access service since such service, "an essential tool in today's workplace," is related or "necessary equipment" authorized by Public Law 104-52. B-308044, Jan. 10, 2007. In doing so, GAO recommended that PTO periodically review the reimbursements to ensure that it has adequate safeguards against private misuse and it is reimbursing employees for home internet service used for official purposes. *Id.*

Page 4-275 – Insert the following after the second full paragraph:

The Department of Homeland Security, Customs and Border Protection (Customs), asked whether it could use its Salaries and Expenses appropriations to pay for relocation expenses its employees who currently reside in Canada or Mexico would incur in order to comply with a new agency directive that their primary residence be in the United States. The employees work at border stations within the United States. In response to heightened security concerns, Customs issued a directive requiring employees assigned to duty stations in the United States to maintain their primary residence in the United States. The Federal Travel Regulation, 41 C.F.R. chs. 300–304, does not address the question of benefits for employees' relocations that do not involve a change in duty station. Recognizing Customs' determination that U.S. residency enables its border workforce to better carry out is mission, GAO determined that Customs' Salaries and Expenses appropriations were available to pay the relocation expenses if the agency chose to do so. B-306748, July 6, 2006.

15. State and Local Taxes

Page 4-286 – Insert the following after the third paragraph:

The complexity can be seen in a 2006 decision in which GAO considered whether a county "surface water management (SWM)" fee was a permissible fee for a service provided or an impermissible tax against the federal government. B-306666, June 5, 2006. A county assessed SWM fees to implement management programs for controlling runoff pollution under the federal Clean Water Act. 33 U.S.C. § 1329. The Clean Water Act also requires federal agencies to comply with state and local water pollution requirements, "including the payment of reasonable service charges." 33 U.S.C. § 1323(a). We concluded that the SWM fee was not a service charge but actually a tax because the county's storm water management was more like a core government service providing undifferentiated benefits to the entire public than a narrowly circumscribed benefit incident to a voluntary act or a service or convenience provided. B-306666, June 5, 2006. Although the Clean Water Act waives sovereign immunity from certain state and local environmental regulations and fees, it does not waive immunity from taxation. Such a waiver must clearly and expressly confer the privilege of taxing the federal government. *Id.* at 11.

Page 4-289 – Replace the second paragraph with the following:

The rule that the government is constitutionally immune from a "vendee tax" but may pay a valid "vendor tax"—even if the government ultimately bears its economic burden—has been recognized and applied in numerous Comptroller General decisions. *E.g.,* B-302230, Dec. 30, 2003; B-288161, Apr. 8, 2002; 46 Comp. Gen. 363 (1966); 24 Comp. Gen. 150 (1944); 23 Comp. Gen. 957 (1944); 21 Comp. Gen. 1119 (1942); 21 Comp. Gen. 733 (1942). The same rule applies to state tax levies on rental fees. *See* 49 Comp. Gen. 204 (1969); B-168593, Jan. 13, 1971; B-170899, Nov. 16, 1970.

Page 4-298 – Replace the first full paragraph with the following:

Naturally, the determination of whether a particular assessment can be paid does not depend on the taxing authority's characterization of the assessment. Thus, payment has been denied where the assessment was termed a "service charge" (B-306666, June 5, 2006), a "benefit assessment" (B-168287, Nov. 9, 1970), a "systems development charge" (B-183094, May 27, 1975), or an "invoice for services" (49 Comp. Gen. 72 (1969)).

Chapter 5

AVAILABILITY OF APPROPRIATIONS: TIME

Page 5-1 – Replace part of the index for section B.1 as follows:

B. THE BONA FIDE NEEDS RULE

1. Background

Page 5-13 – Replace the first full paragraph with the following:

While the rule itself is universally applicable, determination of what constitutes a *bona fide* need of a particular fiscal year depends largely on the facts and circumstances of the particular case. B-308010, Apr. 20, 2007; 70 Comp. Gen. 469, 470 (1991); 44 Comp. Gen. 399, 401 (1965); 37 Comp. Gen. at 159.

Page 5-15 – Insert the following new section c., including the references to new footnote numbers 8a, 8b, 8c, and 8d, after the first full paragraph:

c. "Parking" or "Banking" Funds

"Parking" or "banking" funds are terms used to describe a transfer of funds to a revolving fund through an interagency agreement in an attempt to keep funds available for new work after the period of availability for those funds expires.[8a] Parking usually occurs when an agency transfers fixed-year funds to a revolving or franchise fund in the mistaken belief that, by doing so, the funds lose their fixed-year character and remain available indefinitely. However, an agency may not extend the availability of its appropriations by transferring them to another agency. B-288142, Sept. 6, 2001. Use of these expired parked funds violates the *bona fide* needs rule. An interagency agreement must be based upon a legitimate, specific, and adequately documented requirement representing a *bona fide* need of the year in which the order is made.

GAO has reported on the parking of funds through interagency agreements, and, over a period of several years, Department of Defense (DOD) officials, including the Comptroller, warned against the misuse of interagency agreements to park or bank funds.[8b] In addition, the Inspectors General for DOD and the Department of the Interior (Interior) have faulted their agencies for misusing interagency transactions in this fashion.[8c] In October 2006, the Treasury issued a bulletin instructing ordering agencies to monitor the activity and age of an interagency order and where there has been no activity for more than 180 days, the ordering agency "shall determine the reasons for the lack of activity on the order." I TFM Bulletin No. 2007-03, Attachment I, ¶ III.B.2 (Oct. 1, 2006).

In a 2007 decision, GAO found that DOD improperly parked funds when it transferred fiscal year appropriations to an Interior franchise fund, GovWorks.[8d] B-308944, July 17, 2007. GovWorks was established to provide common administrative services to Interior and other agencies by procuring goods and services from vendors on behalf of federal agencies on a competitive basis. DOD used Military Interdepartmental Purchase Requests (MIPRs) to transfer funds to GovWorks but did not identify the specific items or services that DOD wanted GovWorks to acquire on its behalf until after the funds had expired. GAO concluded that DOD had improperly parked funds with GovWorks by transferring funds from one fiscal year for use by GovWorks for goods and services after the period of availability for those funds had expired. GAO pointed out that, by doing so, "officials of both agencies acted in disregard of . . . the *bona fide* needs rule." *Id.* at 13.

Page 5-15 – Insert the following as new footnote number 8a:

[8a] DOD, Undersecretary of Defense, Comptroller, Memorandum for the Assistant Secretary of the Army (Financial Management and Comptroller), *et al., Proper Use of Interagency Agreements for Non-Department of Defense Contracts Under Authorities Other than the Economy Act,* Mar. 24, 2005 (2005 DOD Memorandum).

Page 5-15 – Insert the following as new footnote number 8b:

[8b] See GAO, Interagency Contracting: Improved Guidance, Planning, and Oversight Would Enable the Department of Homeland Security to Address Risks, GAO-06-996 (Washington, D.C.: Sept. 27, 2006); Improper Use of Industrial Funds By Defense Extended the Life of Appropriations Which Otherwise Would Have Expired, GAO/AFMD-84-34 (Washington, D.C.: June 5, 1984); 2005 DOD Memorandum; DOD, Undersecretary of Defense, Memorandum for the Chairman of the Joint Chiefs of Staff, et al., Fiscal Principles and Interagency Agreements, Sept. 25, 2003.

Page 5-15 – Insert the following as new footnote number 8c:

[8c] DOD, Office of Inspector General, FY 2005 DOD Purchases Made Through the Department of the Interior, No. D-2007-044 (Jan. 16, 2007); Interior, Office of the Inspector General, FY 2005 Department of the Interior Expenses Made on Behalf of the Department of Defense, No. X-IN-MOA-0018-2005 (Jan. 9, 2007).

Page 5-15 – Insert the following as new footnote number 8d:

[8d] GovWorks is officially known as the Acquisition Services Directorate. *See* www.govworks.gov (last visited Feb. 8, 2008).

2. Future Years' Needs

Page 5-17 – Insert the following after the first partial paragraph:

An interesting situation involving a contract with renewable options arose in B-308026, Sept. 14, 2006. The National Labor Relations Board (NLRB) entered into a contract with Electronic Data Systems for the acquisition of ongoing operational and technical support for its automated Case Activity Tracking System. The contract's initial performance period was October 1, 2001, through September 30, 2002, with options through September 30, 2015. On September 30, 2005, NLRB exercised option four, specifying a performance period of October 1, 2005, through September 30, 2006, and charged the obligation to its fiscal year 2005 appropriation. In a June 2006 report, the NLRB Inspector General concluded that NLRB had improperly obligated its fiscal year 2005 appropriation because obligating the fiscal year 2005 appropriation for the performance of severable services that would occur entirely in fiscal year 2006 was a violation of the *bona fide* needs rule. The Inspector General said that NLRB should charge the obligation against its fiscal year 2006 appropriation. NLRB proposed to remedy its improper obligation by modifying the contract to have the performance period of the contract run from September 30, 2005, through September 29, 2006, instead of October 1, 2005, through September 30, 2006. NLRB explained that it had intended a performance period commencing September 30, 2005, but due to an inadvertent ministerial error this was not reflected in the contract. GAO agreed with the Inspector General. GAO said that, given the terms of the contract, NLRB had incurred an obligation against its fiscal year 2006 appropriation and that NLRB should adjust its accounts accordingly. NLRB could not remedy its improper obligation by adjusting its contract's performance period instead of its accounts.

> "It is one thing for an agency to take full advantage of available appropriations, maximizing the effectiveness of federal funds entrusted to its use; it is quite another thing, however, for an agency to alter executed contracts in order to reach expired funds—funds that Congress appropriated for agency programs and activities of the previous fiscal year. That is what NLRB proposes to do. Were NLRB to adjust the fourth option's performance period, its sole reason for doing so would be to reach fiscal year 2005 appropriations because, in September 2005, that is what NLRB had intended to do. However, NLRB's fiscal year 2005 appropriation has expired.
>
> ". . . Instead of adjusting its obligations to reflect what actually occurred, NLRB would revise what actually occurred so that it can finance option four with fiscal year 2005 funds. . . . The account adjustment authority of [31 U.S.C. § 1553(a)] is not a palliative for errors of this sort."

B-308026, Sept. 14, 2006, at 5–6 (footnote omitted).

Page 5-17 – Insert the following after the first full paragraph:

In 2007, GAO considered how this related to seven end-of-the-fiscal year subscription renewals. The National Labor Relations Board (NLRB) purchased seven Web site database subscriptions to support the work of its attorneys and other professionals. B-309530, Sept. 17, 2007. In September 2006, NLRB placed orders to renew each of these subscriptions with the respective vendors, stating that it needed to have the orders placed for the renewal before the existing subscriptions expired in order to ensure uninterrupted delivery. Each order placed was for a period of 1 year beginning on the day following the expiration of the existing subscription and, for each, the agency obligated its fiscal year 2006 annual appropriation. For five subscriptions, the performance period was from October 1, 2006, to September 30, 2007; for two subscriptions, the performance period was from November 1, 2006, to October 31, 2007. *Id.* GAO determined that NLRB did not violate the *bona fide* needs rule for the five Web site database subscription renewals that it needed to have in place on October 1, 2006, the first day of fiscal year 2007. Even though delivery of the renewed subscriptions would occur entirely in fiscal year 2007, NLRB reasonably determined that the renewal orders needed to be placed in fiscal year 2006 to ensure continued receipt of the subscriptions past the expiration of the existing subscriptions on September 30, 2006. *Id.* However, NLRB violated the *bona fide* needs rule when it obligated fiscal year 2006 funds to renew the two Web site database subscriptions that were not due to expire until October 31, 2006. These subscription renewals were a *bona fide* need of fiscal year 2007 for which fiscal year 2007 appropriations should have been used. *Id.*

5. Services Rendered beyond the Fiscal Year

Page 5-24 – Replace the second paragraph after the quote with the following:

The rationale of 23 Comp. Gen. 370 was applied in 59 Comp. Gen. 386 (1980) (requisition for printing accompanied by manuscript sufficient for Government Printing Office to proceed with job). *See, e.g.,* 65 Comp. Gen. 741 (1986) (contract for study and final report on psychological problems among Vietnam veterans); B-257977, Nov. 15, 1995 (contract for 2-year intern training program since interns are required to complete entire training program to be eligible for noncompetitive Presidential Management Intern appointment). *See also* B-305484, June 2, 2006 (appointment of an arbitrator to hear a case is in the nature of a nonseverable service and the National Mediation Board should record an obligation of the current appropriation based on the estimated cost of paying the arbitrator to submit an award); 73 Comp. Gen. 77 (1994) (subsequent modifications to Fish and Wildlife Service research work orders should be charged to the fiscal year current when the work orders were issued since the purpose of the research is to provide a final research report and the services under the contract are nonseverable). The last two decisions are noteworthy because they pointed out that limitation of funds clauses or subject to availability clauses do not affect the application of the *bona fide* needs rule and the severable test. B-305484; 73 Comp. Gen. at 80.

8. Multiyear Contracts

Page 5-41 – Replace the first full paragraph with the following:

If an agency is contracting with fiscal year appropriations and does not have multiyear contracting authority, one course of action, apart from a series of separate fiscal year contracts, is a fiscal year contract with renewal options, with each renewal option (1) contingent on the availability of future appropriations and (2) to be exercised only by affirmative action on the part of the government (as opposed to automatic renewal unless the government refuses). *Leiter v. United States,* 271 U.S. 204 (1926); 66 Comp. Gen. 556 (1987); 36 Comp. Gen. 683 (1957); 33 Comp. Gen. 90 (1953); 29 Comp. Gen. 91 (1949); 28 Comp. Gen. 553 (1949); B-88974, Nov. 10, 1949. The inclusion of a renewal option is key; with a renewal option, the government incurs a financial obligation only for the fiscal year, and incurs no financial obligation for subsequent years unless and until it exercises its right to renew. The government records the amount of its obligation for the first fiscal year against the appropriation current at the time it awards the contract. The government also records amounts of obligations for future fiscal years against appropriations current at the time it exercises its renewal options. The mere inclusion of a contract provision conditioning the government's obligation on future appropriations without also subjecting the multiyear contract to the government's renewal option each year would be insufficient. *Cray Research, Inc. v. United States,* 44 Fed. Cl. 327, 332 (1999). Thus, in 42 Comp. Gen. 272 (1962), the Comptroller General, while advising the Air Force that under the circumstances it could complete that particular contract, also advised that the proper course of action would be either to use an annual contract with renewal options or to obtain specific multiyear authority from Congress. *Id.* at 278.

Page 5-43 – Insert the following after the quoted language in the first partial paragraph:

Another course of action for an agency with fiscal year money to cover possible needs beyond that fiscal year is an indefinite- delivery/indefinite-quantity (IDIQ) contract. An IDIQ contract is a form of an indefinite-quantity contract, which provides for an indefinite quantity of supplies or services, within stated limits, during a fixed period. 48 C.F.R. § 16.504(a). Under an IDIQ contract, actual quantities and delivery dates remain undefined until the agency places a task or delivery order under the contract. When an agency executes an indefinite-quantity contract such as an IDIQ contract, the agency must record an obligation in the amount of the required minimum purchase. At the time of award, the government commits itself to purchase only a minimum amount of supplies or services and has a fixed liability for the amount to which it committed itself. *See* 48 C.F.R. §§ 16.501-2(b)(3) and 16.504(a)(1). The agency has no liability beyond its minimum commitment unless and until it places additional orders. An agency is required to record an obligation at the time it incurs a legal liability. 65 Comp. Gen. 4, 6 (1985); B-242974.6, Nov. 26, 1991. Therefore, for an IDIQ contract, an agency must record an obligation for the minimum amount at the time of contract execution. In B-302358, Dec. 27, 2004, GAO determined that the Bureau of Customs and Border Protection's (Customs) Automated Commercial Environment contract was an IDIQ contract. As such, Customs incurred a legal liability of $25 million for its minimum contractual commitment at the time of contract award. However, Customs failed to record its $25 million obligation until 5 months after contract award. GAO determined that to be consistent with the recording statute, 31 U.S.C. § 1501(a)(1), Customs should have recorded an obligation for the contract minimum of $25 million against a currently available appropriation for the authorized purpose at the time the IDIQ contract was awarded.

9. Specific Statutcs Providing for Multiyear and Other Contracting Authorities

Page 5-46 – Replace the third full paragraph with the following:

The Federal Acquisition Streamlining Act of 1994 (FASA) and related statutes extended multiyear contracting authority with annual funds to nonmilitary departments.[30] FASA authorizes an executive agency to enter into a multiyear contract for the acquisition of property or services for more than 1, but not more than 5 years, if the agency makes certain administrative determinations. 41 U.S.C. § 254c. Related laws extend this authority to various legislative branch agencies.[31] Through FASA and the related laws, Congress has relaxed the constraints of the *bona fide* needs rule by giving agencies the flexibility to structure contracts to fund the obligations up front, incrementally, or by using the standard *bona fide* needs rule approach. B-277165, Jan. 10, 2000. To the extent an agency elects to obligate a 5-year contract incrementally, it must also obligate termination costs. *Cf.* B-302358, Dec. 27, 2004 (since the contract at issue was an indefinite-delivery/indefinite-quantity contract, it was not subject to the requirements of 41 U.S.C. § 254c and the agency did not need to obligate estimated termination costs at the time of contract award).

C. Advance Payments

1. The Statutory Prohibition

Page 5-53 – *Insert the following before the first full paragraph:*

Another example of a statutory exception was considered in B-306975, Feb. 27, 2006. The National Archives and Records Administration (NARA) stores temporary and pre-archival records that belong to it and other federal agencies in its Records Center Programs Facilities. Other federal agencies may enter into agreements with NARA to transfer and store records at the NARA records centers. The Treasury and General Appropriations Act, 2000, established the Records Center Revolving Fund to pay for expenses and equipment necessary to provide the storage and authorized agencies to make advance payments to the Revolving Fund. Pub. L. No. 106-58, title IV, 113 Stat. 430, 460–61 (Sept. 29, 1999). GAO had no objection, therefore, to NARA's proposal to bill its customers at the beginning of each month based on its estimate of services it will provide that month and to adjust the next month's bill to reflect actual costs of services rendered. However, if a customer advances fiscal year funds for September's estimated costs, NARA may not credit excess amounts in adjusting October's bill but rather must return the excess to the customers. These funds would not be available for obligation of the next fiscal year commencing October 1. Likewise, if a customer agency owes more than the amount advanced in September, the customer must cover the underpayment from the previous fiscal year's funds, B-306975, Feb. 27, 2006.

D. Disposition of Appropriation Balances

3. Expired Appropriations Accounts

Page 5-72 – Replace the second full paragraph with the following:

During the 5-year period, the expired account balance may be used to liquidate obligations properly chargeable to the account prior to its expiration.[50] The expired account balance also remains available to make legitimate obligation adjustments, that is, to record previously unrecorded obligations and to make upward adjustments in previously under recorded obligations. For example, Congress appropriated funds to provide education benefits to veterans under the so-called "GI bill," codified at 38 U.S.C. § 1662. Prior to the expiration of the appropriation, the Veterans Administration (VA) denied the benefits to certain Vietnam era veterans. The denial was appealed to the courts. The court determined that certain veterans may have been improperly denied benefits and ordered VA to entertain new applications and reconsider the eligibility of veterans to benefits. VA appealed the court order. Prior to a final resolution of the issue, the appropriation expired. GAO determined that, consistent with 31 U.S.C. § 1502(b),[51] the unobligated balance of VA's expired appropriation was available to pay benefits to veterans who filed applications prior to the expiration of the appropriation or who VA determined were improperly denied education benefits. 70 Comp. Gen. 225 (1991). For a further discussion of the availability of funds between expiration and closing of an account, see B-301561, June 14, 2004 and B-265901, Oct. 14, 1997.

Page 5-72 – Replace the last partial paragraph with the following:

Unobligated balances in the expired account cannot be used to satisfy an obligation properly chargeable to current appropriations (B-308944, July 17, 2007; 50 Comp. Gen. 863 (1971)), or to any other expired account.[52] *See* Chapter 5, section B.1.c. The authority of 31 U.S.C. § 1553(a) is intended to permit agencies to adjust their accounts to more accurately reflect obligations and liabilities actually incurred during the period of availability. 63 Comp. Gen. 525, 528 (1984). However, arbitrary deobligation in reliance upon the authority to make subsequent adjustments is not consistent with the statutory purpose. B-179708, July 10, 1975.

4. Closed Appropriation Accounts

Page 5-73 – Replace the third full paragraph with the following: Once an account has been closed:

> "[O]bligations and adjustments to obligations that would have been properly chargeable to that account, both as to purpose and in amount, before closing and that are not otherwise chargeable to any current appropriation account of the agency may be charged to any current appropriation account of the agency available for the same purpose."

31 U.S.C. § 1553(b)(1). *See also* B-301561, June 14, 2004.

5. Exemptions from the Account Closing Procedures

Page 5-76 – Replace the second full paragraph with the following:

To the extent of its applicability, the statutory scheme found at 31 U.S.C. §§ 1551–1558 provides the exclusive method for the payment of obligations chargeable to expired appropriations. B-101860, Dec. 5, 1963. Thus, there is generally no authority to transfer appropriations to some form of trust fund or working fund for the purpose of preserving their availability. *Id.*; B-308944, July 17, 2007 (the Department of Defense transferred fiscal year funds to a franchise fund in an attempt to impermissibly extend the funds' availability). *See* Chapter 5, section B.1.c. See also 31 U.S.C. § 1532, which prohibits the transfer of appropriations to a working fund without statutory authority. In B-288142, Sept. 6, 2001, customer agencies made advances from their fixed period appropriations to the Library of Congress for deposit to the credit of the no-year FEDLINK revolving fund. The advances were used by the Library of Congress to pay the cost of service provided to the agencies by Library of Congress contractors. Once the service was provided and the cost determined, the Library discovered that some agencies had advanced amounts in excess of the cost of the service ordered. We determined that the Library of Congress lacked authority to apply the excess amount to pay for orders for service placed after the expiration of the fixed period appropriation charged with the advance.

VOLUME 2

Chapter 6

AVAILABILITY OF APPROPRIATIONS: AMOUNT

B. TYPES OF APPROPRIATION LANGUAGE

1. Lump-Sum Appropriations

Page 6-6 – Replace the last partial paragraph with the following:

The answer to these questions is one of the most important principles of appropriations law. The rule, simply stated, is this: Restrictions on a lump-sum appropriation contained in the agency's budget request or in legislative history are not legally binding on the department or agency unless they are carried into (specified in) the appropriation act itself, or unless some other statute restricts the agency's spending flexibility. *See Hein v. Freedom From Religion Foundation, Inc.*, ___ U.S. ___, 127 S. Ct. 2553, 2568 n.7 (2007) and cases cited. This is an application of the fundamental principle of statutory construction that legislative is not law and carries no legal significance unless "anchored in the text of the statute." *Shannon v. United States*, 512 U.S. 573, 583 (1994).[5] Of course, the agency cannot exceed the total amount of the lump-sum appropriation, and its spending must not violate other applicable statutory restrictions.[6] The rule applies equally whether the legislative history is mere acquiescence in the agency's budget request or an affirmative expression of intent.

Page 6-20 – Replace the first full paragraph with the following:

The Court noted that while the agency had repeatedly informed Congress about the program in question, "as we have explained, these representations do not translate through the medium of legislative history into legally binding obligations." *Id.* at 194. Subsequent judicial decisions have, of course, followed this approach. *E.g., Hein v. Freedom From Religion Foundation, Inc.,* ___ U.S. ___, 127 S. Ct. 2553, 2568 n.7

(2007); *State of California v. United States,* 104 F.3d 1086, 1093–94 (9th Cir.), *cert. denied,* 522 U.S. 806 (1997); *State of New Jersey v. United States,* 91 F.3d 463, 470–71 (3rd Cir. 1996); *Vizenor v. Babbitt,* 927 F. Supp. 1193 (D. Minn. 1996); *Allred v. United States,* 33 Fed. Cl. 349 (1995). *But see Ramah Navajo School Board, Inc. v. Babbitt,* 87 F.3d 1338 (D.C. Cir. 1996).[19]

C. The Antideficiency Act

2. Obligation/Expenditure in Excess or Advance of Appropriations

Page 6-39 – Replace the first full paragraph with the following:

Some government corporations are also classified as agencies of the United States government, and their officials are therefore "officers and employees of the United States." To the extent they operate with funds which are regarded as appropriated funds, they too are subject to 31 U.S.C. § 1341(a)(1). *E.g.,* B-223857, Feb. 27, 1987 (Commodity Credit Corporation); B-135075-O.M., Feb. 14, 1975 (Inter-American Foundation). It follows that section 1341(a)(1) does not apply to a corporation that, although established by federal statute, is not an agency of the United States government. *E.g.,* B-308037, Sept. 14, 2006 (Legal Services Corporation); B-175155-O.M., July 26, 1976 (Amtrak). These principles are, of course, subject to variation if and to the extent provided in the relevant organic legislation.

Page 6-40 – Insert the following after the first full paragraph:

In B-308715, Apr. 20, 2007, the Department of Energy (DOE) violated the Antideficiency Act when it obligated and spent appropriated funds in advance and in excess of available appropriations. DOE is statutorily barred from using any funds provided by Energy and Water Development appropriation acts "to implement or finance authorized . . . loan guarantee programs unless specific provision is made for such programs in an appropriation Act." 42 U.S.C. § 7278. DOE used 2006 and 2007 appropriations for a loan guarantee program even though Congress had not enacted the appropriations for that purpose. Consequently, DOE violated the Antideficiency Act, as well as the purpose statute, 31 U.S.C. § 1301(a) (appropriation "shall be applied only to the objects for which the appropriations were made"), discussed in Chapter 4.

Page 6-48 – Replace the first paragraph with the following:

To illustrate, an agency's acceptance of an offer to install automatic telephone equipment for $40,000 when the unobligated balance in the relevant appropriation was only $20,000 violated the Antideficiency Act. 35 Comp. Gen. 356 (1955). In addition, when other legislation limits the availability of an appropriation, the agency may not exceed the limitation. In B-307720, Sept. 27, 2007, the Department of Agriculture made payments to participants of the Conservation Security Program in excess of annual limits on such payments imposed by the program's authorizing legislation, 16 U.S.C. § 3838–3838c. Notwithstanding that the amount of the department's appropriation was adequate otherwise to cover the amount of the payments, the department could not ignore the statutory limitation on such payments. *Id.*

Page 6-53 – Replace the last paragraph with the following:

Importantly, FASA does not apply to all contracts that are intended to meet the needs of more than one fiscal year. Obviously, if multiple year or no-year appropriations are legally available for the full contract period, an agency need not rely on FASA. Also, certain contract forms do not constitute multiyear contracts within the scope of FASA. For example, in B-302358, Dec. 27, 2004, GAO determined that a Bureau of Customs and Border Protection procurement constituted an "indefinite-delivery, indefinite-quantity" (IDIQ) contract that was not subject to FASA. The decision explained that, unlike a contract covered by FASA, an IDIQ contract does not obligate the government beyond its initial year. Rather, it obligates the government only to order a minimum amount of supplies or services. The cost of that minimum amount is recorded as an obligation against the appropriation current when the contract is entered into.[54] *See also* B-308969, May 31, 2007 (agency failed to obligate the entire minimum amount of an IDIQ contract against the appropriated funds for the fiscal year in which the contract was awarded).

Page 6-70 – Insert the following after the first full paragraph:

The Court of Federal Claims applied the rule against open-ended indemnity agreements in a 2007 case involving a mushroom grower seeking indemnification from the government for losses it had incurred as a result of operating a defective waste facility that had been designed by the Department of Agriculture's National Resource Conservation Service (NRCS). *Rick's Mushroom Service, Inc. v. United States,* 76 Fed. Cl. 250 (2007). Pursuant to a cooperative agreement with NRCS, the facility had been constructed in accordance with detailed plans and specifications drafted by NRCS. The plaintiff argued that the cooperative agreement was a contract that created an implied warranty under the rule known as the *Spearin* doctrine. The government asserted that the Antideficiency Act precludes any employee of the NRCS from possessing the authority to bind the government to "an open-ended indemnity contract in the absence of specific authorization for the undertaking." *Id.* at 260. The government cited to the statement in *Hercules,* 516 U.S. at 427–28, that "the contracting officer's presumed knowledge of [the Antideficiency Act's] prohibition [is] strong evidence that the officer would not have provided, in fact, the contractual indemnification claimed." The Federal Claims court in *Rick's Mushroom* agreed, noting that the Supreme Court in *Hercules* relied upon the fact that the Comptroller General has repeatedly ruled that government procurement agencies may not enter into the type of open-ended indemnity for third-part liability that petitioner claims to have implicitly received. *Rick's Mushroom,* 76 Fed. Cl. at 260.

Page 6-83 – Replace the first full paragraph with the following:

More recent GAO decisions likewise consistently apply the principle that the use of appropriated funds for unauthorized or prohibited purposes violates the Antideficiency Act (absent an alternative funding source) since zero funds are available for that purpose. B-302710, May 19, 2004 (use of funds in violation of statutory prohibition against publicity or propaganda); B-300325, Dec. 13, 2002 (appropriations used for unauthorized technical assistance purposes); B-300192, Nov. 13, 2002 (violation of appropriation rider prohibiting use of funds to implement an Office of Management and Budget memorandum); B-290005, July 1, 2002 (appropriation used to procure unauthorized legal services); 71 Comp. Gen. 402, 406 (1992) (unauthorized use of Training and Employment Services appropriation); B-246304, July 31, 1992 (potential violation of appropriation act "Buy American" provision); B-248284, Sept. 1, 1992 (nondecision letter) (reprogramming of funds to an unauthorized purpose). *Cf.* B-309181, Aug. 17, 2007 (although the Department of Defense, without a delegation of lease authority from the General Services Administration, improperly entered into a lease, it did not incur an Antideficiency Act violation because it had an appropriation available to make lease payments).

3. Voluntary Services Prohibition

Page 6-102 – Insert the following after the first paragraph:

An interesting 2007 case explored the applicability of the voluntary services prohibition in the context of a recess appointment. B-309301, June 8, 2007. Exercising his constitutional power to make a recess appointment, the President appointed an individual as ambassador to Belgium whose nomination to that same position he had previously withdrawn from Senate consideration. The individual was denied a salary by the State Department under 5 U.S.C. § 5503, which prohibits payment for services—

> "to an individual appointed during a recess of the Senate to fill a vacancy in an existing office, if the vacancy existed while the Senate was in session and was by law required to be filled by and with the advice and consent of the Senate, until the appointee has been confirmed by the Senate."

Nonetheless, the individual was willing to serve as ambassador, which raised the question of whether the State Department could accept the uncompensated services he was willing to provide. GAO noted that the voluntary services prohibition was enacted to prevent coercive deficiencies and future equitable claims against the government. Since there was a statutory prohibition barring the State Department from paying his salary, this was not a situation in which a coercive deficiency might occur. Similar to the situation in which an individual gratuitously waives his salary in advance, the recess appointee accepted the position knowing that he would not receive compensation for his services. *Id.* Even if he were to file a claim against the government for compensation, there is a statutory prohibition to payment of his salary. 5 U.S.C. § 5503. Therefore, the voluntary services prohibition did not apply in this situation, and the Department of State could allow him to serve as ambassador to Belgium without compensation. GAO stated: "We are also led to this interpretation by the fact that serious constitutional issues would arise if section 5503, in conjunction with the voluntary services prohibition, were read to directly restrict the President from making a recess appointment." B-309301, at 6.

Page 6-110 – Insert the following after the first partial paragraph (between "Id. at 7" and "d. Exceptions"):

In a similar case, GAO was asked to review a model no-cost contract offered by National Conference Services, Inc. (NCSI) for conference, event, and trade show planning services. The proposed NCSI contract provided:

> "The Contractor [NCSI] may choose to provide for all services as required by the task order at no cost to the Government. The Contractor is entitled to all of the registration, exhibition, sponsorship and/or other fees collected as payment for performance under the task order if there is no cost to the Government. In this case, the Contractor is liable for all costs related to the performance of the task order as defined in the task order and the government's liability for payment of services under this task order is 'zero.'"

B-308968, Nov. 27, 2007, at 2. GAO found that an agency agreeing to these terms would have no financial liability to NCSI, nor would NCSI have any expectation of payment from the government. Applying the same analysis as in the GSA case, GAO determined that an agency entering into the NCSI contract would neither augment its appropriation nor run afoul of the voluntary services prohibition. GAO advised that there are other considerations beyond compliance with fiscal laws that an agency should take into account before agreeing to a no-cost contract such as the one proffered by NCSI, including weighing the value of the services received from the contractor with that of the concession given to the contractor. For example, an agency should consider the ultimate cost to the government as a whole when most attendees are expected to be government employees. Agency officials also should consider possible conflicts of interest before signing a no-cost contract, keeping in mind that control of the agenda, selection of speakers, and other matters concerning content should serve the government's, not the contractor's, purpose. In addition, agencies should ensure an open, transparent selection process before entering into no-cost contracts. GAO said, "Ultimately, an agency must not lose sight of its objectives for a particular event and should ensure that in avoiding costs to the agency, it does not take actions that compromise the effectiveness of its conference, undermine the achievement of agency goals, or violate ethics rules." *Id.* at 5–6.

5. Penalties and Reporting Requirements

Page 6-146 – Replace the first full paragraph and insert new footnote number 138a as follows:

What if GAO uncovers a violation but the agency thinks GAO is wrong? The agency must still make the required reports, and must include an explanation of its disagreement. OMB Cir. No. A-11, § 145. *See also* GAO, *Anti-Deficiency Act: Agriculture's Food and Nutrition Service Violates the*

Anti-Deficiency Act, GAO/AFMD-87-20 (Washington, D.C.: Mar. 17, 1987). Should an agency fail to make the required report within a reasonable period of time, GAO will advise Congress that the agency violated the Antideficiency Act but has not yet reported the violation. *See* B-308715, Nov. 13, 2007.[138a]

Page 6-146 – Insert the following as new footnote number 138a:

[138a] GAO advised Congress that the Department of Energy (DOE) had violated the Antideficiency Act in fiscal years 2006 and 2007 but had not reported the violations to Congress more than 6 months after GAO found the violations. Subsequently, 2 months after GAO notified Congress, the department made the required reports and provided copies to GAO. Letter from Samuel W. Bodman, Secretary, DOE, to David M. Walker, Comptroller General of the United States, Jan. 14, 2008.

E. Augmentation of Appropriations

2. Disposition of Moneys Received: Repayments and Miscellaneous Receipts

Page 6-172 – Insert the following after the first full paragraph:

In B-305402, Jan. 3, 2006, GAO refused to classify as a refund an amount that did not represent the return of an overpayment to the agency. That case concerned the proper treatment of demutualization compensation that the National Aeronautics and Space Administration (NASA) received from its contractor, California Institute of Technology (Caltech). Caltech had received the demutualization compensation in the form of stock as a policyholder of Prudential Life Insurance Company policies that Caltech held for some employees operating the Jet Propulsion Laboratory for NASA. Caltech notified NASA of the compensation, and NASA instructed Caltech to liquidate the stock and place the proceeds in an interest-bearing account. GAO found that these proceeds do not constitute a refund that NASA could credit to its appropriation because they do not represent a repayment of funds that were "in excess of what was actually due"; that is, the proceeds do not reflect a repayment from Caltech of an amount that NASA had previously overpaid Caltech. At the time NASA paid allocable costs of the defined benefit retirement plan, the amounts were correct, and the fact that the moneys NASA received as a result of the demutualization are related to the terminated retirement plans does not make the proceeds a refund. Since the demutualization compensation cannot be properly characterized as a refund, the proceeds from the sale of the demutualization compensation must be deposited in the general fund of the Treasury as miscellaneous receipts. *Id.*

Page 6-176 – Replace fourth full paragraph with the following:

The deposit timing requirements of 31 U.S.C. § 3302(c) and the implementing Treasury regulations apply as well when public moneys are held by nonfederal custodians. Thus, GAO found that these requirements were violated where the Department of Veterans Affairs (VA) allowed contractors to hold payments it collected on VA loans in an interest-bearing account for 30 days or more before transferring the payments to the Treasury. *See* GAO, *Internal Controls: VA Lacked Accountability Over Its Direct Loan and Loan Sale Activities,* GAO/AIMD-99-24 (Washington, D.C.: Mar. 24, 1999), at 16–18. *See also* B-305402, Jan. 3, 2006 (the National Aeronautics and Space Administration should have deposited amounts received from its contractor in the Treasury the day following the receipt of those amounts).

Page 6-177 – Replace the partial paragraph after the quoted language with the following:

B-303413, Nov. 8, 2004. See also B-300826, Mar. 3, 2005, at 6, noting that an agency cannot avoid section 3302(b) by authorizing a contractor to charge fees to outside parties and keep the payments in order to offset costs that would otherwise be borne by agency appropriations. The decision in B-300826 was affirmed in B-306663, Jan. 4, 2006. *See also* B-307137, July 12, 2006 (the Department of Energy (DOE) violated 31 U.S.C. § 3302(b) and augmented its appropriations when it authorized the United States Enrichment Corporation to hold, invest, and use the proceeds from public sales of government-owned uranium on behalf of DOE prior to the enactment of specific statutory authority exempting the proceeds of those uranium sales from section 3302(b)).

Page 6-183 – Insert the following after the first full paragraph:

A recent situation involved fees collected by a government corporation. Congress established the State Justice Institute as a private, nonprofit corporation to further "the development and adoption of improved judicial administration in State courts in the United States." 42 U.S.C. § 10702(a). Although the Institute receives an annual appropriation from Congress, the Institute is not a government agency or instrumentality except for limited purposes specified in its authorizing statute, and its employees are not to be considered employees of the United States. 42 U.S.C. § 10704. The Executive Director of the Institute asked whether the Institute could retain fees the Institute obtains for the use of advertising space in its semiannual newsletter, or whether the fees must be treated as miscellaneous receipts under 31 U.S.C. § 3302(b) and deposited in the Treasury. The Institute is not a government agency, and GAO stated that "[a]lthough Congress imposed on the Institute certain requirements typically applicable to a federal agency, it did so selectively, against the general backdrop of a private corporate entity. 42 U.S.C. § 10702(a)." B-307317, Sept. 13, 2006, at 3. GAO found nothing explicitly or implicitly in the Institute's authorizing statute that would suggest or require application of the miscellaneous receipts statute to the Institute. Therefore, GAO concluded that in accepting the advertising fees the Institute was not "receiving money for the Government," and so the Institute could retain the fees without violating the miscellaneous receipts statute. *Id.* (GAO cautioned, however, that in retaining such fees the Institute should be cognizant of the legal constraints and policy considerations regarding advertising it chooses to carry).

Page 6-197 – Replace the last partial paragraph with the following:

The decision in B-302962 held that the exception to the interdepartmental waiver doctrine applied in the case of damage to facilities of the National Archives and Records Administration (NARA) whose operations were financed by a revolving fund. Thus, NARA should collect from other federal agencies, their contractors, or NARA's own contractors, as the case may be, amounts sufficient to repair damages they caused to NARA's facilities and deposit those amounts into the revolving fund.

In other circumstances, however, GAO concluded that NARA's funds were available to cover the damage. In B-308822, May 2, 2007, a building failure caused water damage to records NARA stored for its federal agency customers in a federal building owned and maintained by the General Services Administration (GSA). Here, the Federal Property Administrative Services Act of 1949, as amended, governs the relationship between GSA and its federal agency customers who occupy GSA-owned and operated buildings. Both GSA's management of federal buildings and NARA records centers operate out of revolving funds. Requiring GSA to reimburse another agency for damages it incurred or reduce the rental charges to cover the damages would reduce amounts available to finance new construction, undermining one of the purposes of the Act. Accordingly, GAO concluded that GSA was not required to reimburse NARA for property damage.

Page 6-199 – Replace the second paragraph with the following:

Federal agencies must have statutory authority both (1) to charge fees for their programs and activities in the first instance and (2), even if they have fee-charging authority, to retain in their appropriations and use the amounts collected. *See, e.g.,* B-306663, Jan. 4, 2006; B-300826, Mar. 3, 2005; B-300248, Jan. 15, 2004. Thus, fees and commissions paid either to the government itself or to a government employee for activities relating to official duties must be deposited in the Treasury as miscellaneous receipts, absent statutory authority to the contrary.

Page 6-199 – Replace the last paragraph with the following:

Of course, if and to the extent expressly authorized by statute an agency may retain fees and use them to offset operating costs. *See, e.g.,* 2 U.S.C. § 68-7(b) (fees and other charges collected for services provided by the Senate Office of Public Records); 7 U.S.C. § 7333(k)(3) (fees for certain services collected by the Commodity Credit Corporation); 10 U.S.C. § 2262 (fees collected from participants to defray Department of Defense costs of hosting conferences); 28 U.S.C. § 1921(e) (fees collected by the United States Marshals Service for service of civil process and judicial execution seizures and sales, to the extent provided in advance in appropriation acts); 28 U.S.C. § 1931 (specified portions of filing fees paid to the clerk of court). The relevant legislation will determine precisely what may be retained. *E.g.,* 34 Comp. Gen. 58 (1954). For example, amounts collected under 10 U.S.C. § 2262 with respect to a Department of Defense-hosted conference can be credited to the appropriation from which the costs of the conference are paid to reimburse the Department for the costs incurred, but if the amount collected ends up being greater than the actual costs of the conference, the excess amount is to be deposited into the Treasury as miscellaneous receipts. 10 U.S.C. §§ 2262(b), (c).

Page 6-212 – Insert the following after the first paragraph:

In B-306860, Feb. 28, 2006, GAO concluded that the terms of a settlement agreement entered into between the Office of Federal Housing Enterprise Oversight (OFHEO) and the Federal Home Loan Mortgage Corporation (Freddie Mac) would not augment OFHEO's appropriation. In this case, the settlement agreement was intended to resolve an administrative proceeding, including production of documents, brought by OFHEO against Freddie Mac pursuant to OFHEO's regulatory oversight authority. As part of the settlement, Freddie Mac agreed to provide the documents and to pay a vendor up to $1 million to electronically format and code certain documents for OFHEO's use. The settlement agreement satisfied a prosecutorial objective, that is, the production of documents, and there was no contractual relationship between OFHEO and the vendor. Instead, the contract was between Freddie Mac and the vendor, and it was Freddie Mac, not OFHEO, who was contractually obligated to pay the vendor. Thus, the costs of formatting the documents were Freddie Mac's costs and not OFHEO's, and Freddie Mac's payment of the formatting costs did not constitute a *de facto* augmentation of OFHEO's appropriation.

The OFHEO decision was explained in B-308476, Dec. 20, 2006, in which GAO determined that the Federal Motor Carrier Safety Administration (FMCSA) did not have authority to retain an award of criminal restitution that a federal district court ordered to be paid to FMCSA. In carrying out its mission to improve the safety of commercial vehicle operations, FMCSA issues and enforces motor carrier safety regulations concerning specified commercial trucking and bus operations. *See* 49 U.S.C. § 113. A trucking company's officers pleaded guilty to violating both the agency regulations and a criminal statute concerning conspiracy to commit false statement offenses. In accepting the plea, the court ordered, among other penalties, the defendants to pay restitution to FMCSA in the amount of $20,000 to compensate FMCSA for the costs of the investigation and prosecution of the case. Unlike the situation in the OFHEO case, if FMCSA retained the $20,000 in restitution, the agency would improperly augment its appropriation. FMCSA receives an appropriation each year to pay for costs of investigations such as the one conducted in the trucking company's case—such costs are necessary expenses of enforcing the agency's safety regulations and are obligations of FMCSA. As such, crediting the restitution award to FMCSA's appropriation would improperly contribute financial resources that supplement those already provided for the agency by Congress. Therefore, FMCSA was required to remit the awarded funds to the Treasury as miscellaneous receipts.

Page 6-214 – Insert the following after the first full bullet at the top of the page:

- Proceeds from the sale of government-owned uranium used to compensate the United States Enrichment Corporation (USEC) for expenses it incurred on behalf of the Department of Energy (DOE). Here, DOE arranged for an independent revenue stream not appropriated to it by Congress; had no authority to retain the proceeds of that revenue stream if received directly; and arranged for its agent, USEC, to receive the proceeds of the unauthorized revenue stream and use those amounts to pay for expenses incurred on behalf of DOE. As DOE's agent, USEC received "money for the government" but failed to deposit the money in the Treasury. Therefore, DOE violated the miscellaneous receipts statute and augmented its appropriations. B-307137, July 12, 2006.

4. Other Augmentation Principles and Cases

Page: 6-239 – Insert the following after the third bullet:

- The Office of Compliance may not accept reimbursements of its costs of investigating and prosecuting alleged violations of section 5 of the Occupational Safety and Health Act (29 U.S.C. § 654), and its costs of monitoring planned abatement actions, from legislative branch agencies since the Office of Compliance receives an annual appropriation to fund these activities. B-308774, Mar. 15, 2007.
- The Pension Benefit Guaranty Corporation may not retain a reimbursement for financial analysis services associated with a request for waiver from claims arising under title IV of the Employee Retirement Income Security Act. B-307849, Mar. 1, 2007. The miscellaneous receipts statute, 31 U.S.C. § 3302(b), requires government corporations to deposit amounts received into the general fund of the Treasury, absent statutory authority to the contrary. *Id.*

Chapter 7

OBLIGATION OF APPROPRIATIONS

B. CRITERIA FOR RECORDING OBLIGATIONS (31 U.S.C. § 1501)

1. Section 1501(a)(1): Contracts

Page 7-21 – Replace first full paragraph with the following:

What does all this signify from the perspective of obligating appropriations? As we noted at the outset, the obligational impact of a variable quantity contract depends on exactly what the government has bound itself to do. A fairly simple generalization can be deduced from the decisions: In a variable quantity contract (requirements or indefinite-quantity), any required minimum purchase must be obligated when the contract is executed; subsequent obligations occur as work orders or delivery orders are placed, and are chargeable to the fiscal year in which the order is placed. B-308969, May 31, 2007 (agency should have obligated the $1 million required minimum purchase under an IDIQ contract against the appropriation for the fiscal year in which the contract was executed). *See also* B-302358, Dec. 27, 2004. Of course, the *bona fide* needs rule applies both at the time the agency enters into the contract and when the agency subsequently places task or work orders.

7. Section 1501(a)(7): Employment and Travel

Page 7-46 – Replace the third paragraph with the following:

For persons compensated on an actual expense basis, it may be necessary to record the obligation as an estimate, to be adjusted when the services are actually performed. Documentation requirements to support the obligation or subsequent claims are up to the agency. For example, the National Mediation Board (NMB) incurs an obligation when it appoints a neutral arbitrator to a grievance adjustment board to hear a specific case or a specified group of related cases. Because NMB does not control the number of days an arbitrator will work before submitting an award, NMB should record an obligation based on its best estimate of the costs of paying the arbitrator and adjust the obligation up or down as more information becomes available. B-305484, June 2, 2006. NMB should liquidate the obligation from the appropriation current at the time NMB incurs the obligation, notwithstanding that the arbitrator's performance may extend into the next fiscal year. *Id.* To the extent GAO indicated in two prior decisions, B-217475, Dec. 24, 1986, and B-217475, May 5, 1986, that NMB may record obligations month-to-month based on the anticipated expenditures it approves in monthly compensation requests, those decisions were overruled by B-305484.

C. Contingent Liabilities

Page 7-56 – Replace the second full paragraph with the following:

Contingent liabilities are not recordable as obligations under section 1501 of title 31.[34] Rather, a contingent liability ripens into a recordable obligation for purposes of section 1501 only if and when the contingency materializes. *E.g.,* B-305484, June 2, 2006; 62 Comp. Gen. 143, 145–46 (1983); 37 Comp. Gen. 691–92 (1958); GAO, *Policy and Procedures Manual for Guidance of Federal Agencies,* title 7, § 3.5.C (Washington, D.C.: May 18, 1993) (hereafter GAO-PPM).

Chapter 8

CONTINUING RESOLUTIONS

B. RATE FOR OPERATIONS

1. Current Rate

Page 8-11 – Insert after the first partial paragraph:

GAO considered the distinction between transferred and reprogrammed funds when calculating the current rate for operations under a continuing resolution at the request of the United States Capitol Police (USCP). Specifically, the USCP asked whether $10 million of unobligated no-year and multiyear balances that it had made available through reprogrammings and transfers to its fiscal year 2006 "General Expenses" appropriation should be included in calculating the current rate under the continuing resolution for its 2007 General Expenses appropriation. USCP had made that amount available for fiscal year 2006 operational needs via a combination of reprogrammings within its General Expenses appropriation and a transfer from its Salaries appropriation to its General Expenses appropriation. GAO stated that in determining the current rate the amount reprogrammed must be distinguished from the amount transferred because reprogrammings and transfers are fundamentally different transactions. A reprogramming is the movement of funds already in an appropriation from one use to another. Unless otherwise restricted by statute, agencies may reprogram funds as they wish to adapt to changing circumstances. Because Congress had already made available the reprogrammed portion of the $10 billion, USCP should consider that amount as part of its current rate under the continuing resolution. In contrast, a transfer is the movement of funds between appropriations, which an agency may do only when Congress grants it the statutory authority to do so. USCP had discretionary authority to transfer funds and used that authority in fiscal year 2006 to transfer the funds from its Salaries appropriation to its General Expenses appropriation. GAO concluded that transfers made at an agency's discretion pursuant to its general transfer authority, and not directed by law, should not be included in the calculation. Therefore, the portion of the $10 million comprised of the transferred funds could not be included in the calculation of the current rate under the continuing resolution. B-308773, Jan. 11, 2007.

Chapter 9

LIABILITY AND RELIEF OF ACCOUNTABLE OFFICERS

B. GENERAL PRINCIPLES

2. Who Is an Accountable Officer?

Page 9-12 – Replace the last paragraph with the following:

In B-280764, GAO did not question the merits of extending accountability and potential pecuniary liability to more Department of Defense (DOD) employees, only the means of accomplishing that objective. In 2002, Congress added new section 2773a to title 10, United States Code, which supplied the department with the requisite statutory authority to designate additional accountable officials.[12] *See* B-305919, Mar. 27, 2006 (DOD may employ foreign local nationals as departmental accountable officials under section 2773a).

C. PHYSICAL LOSS OR DEFICIENCY

2. Who Can Grant Relief?

Page 9-40 –Replace footnote 27 with the following:

[27] As noted earlier in section B.2 of this chapter, the Department of Defense (DOD) has been given the authority to hold other "departmental accountable officers," besides certifying and disbursing officers, liable financially for illegal or erroneous payments resulting from their negligence.

10 U.S.C. § 2773a. *Cf.* B-305919, Mar. 27, 2006 (foreign local nationals may serve as DOD accountable officials under 10 U.S.C. § 2773a, even though they may not be subject to pecuniary liability under United States law, because of U.S. agreements with foreign governments). This would include employees whose duty it was to provide information, data, or services that are directly relied upon by a certifying official in the certification of vouchers for payment.

Page 9-43 – Replace the first paragraph with the following:

As noted above and in sections B.2 and C.1.b of this chapter, the statutory scheme for military accountable officers was changed by section 913 of Public Law No. 104-106, div. A, title IX, subtitle B, 110 Stat. 186, 410–12 (Feb. 10, 1996). Section 913 amended a number of provisions in titles 10, 31, and 37 of the United States Code to authorize the designation and appointment of certifying and disbursing officials within the Department of Defense (DOD) (including military departments, defense agencies, and field activities) to clearly delineate a separation of duties and accountabilities between personnel who authorize payments (certifying officers) and personnel who make payments (disbursing officers). In doing so, section 913 also amended 31 U.S.C. § 3527(b) to apply to all accountable officials of the armed forces, not just disbursing officers,[31] and included a new section 3527(b)(1)(B) to provide relief for erroneous payments made by military accountable officials. As in the case of a physical loss or deficiency, the finding of the Secretary involved regarding whether the circumstances warrant relief is conclusive on the Comptroller General. In B-307693, Apr. 12, 2007, GAO addressed whether the limitation in 31 U.S.C. § 3527 applies to requests from certifying officers of DOD components other than the armed services for relief of erroneous payments under the revised section 3527(b). GAO determined that, because the term "armed forces" as used in section 3527(b) applies only to the Army, Navy, Air Force, or Marine Corps, GAO may entertain relief requests from certifying officers of other DOD components in the same manner as it does requests from certifying officers in other agencies. Thus, GAO considered the request of a certifying officer of the Defense Logistics Agency, an agency of DOD but not one of the armed forces, in B-307693.

D. ILLEGAL OR IMPROPER PAYMENT

2. Certifying Officers

Page 9-91 – Replace the last paragraph with the following:

Whatever else the certifying officer's verification burden may or may not involve, it certainly involves questioning items on the face of vouchers or supporting documents, which simply do not look right. A critical tool that certifying officers have to carry out their responsibility is the power to question, and refuse certification of, payments that may be improper. *See, e.g.,* B-303177, Oct. 20, 2004. For example, GAO considered the propriety of imposing liability on a certifying officer who certified payment of a purchase card billing statement that included improper purchase card transactions. B-307693,. Apr. 12, 2007. GAO found that, to execute his statutory responsibility properly and to avoid possible pecuniary liability, the certifying officer should have scrutinized the billing statement and disputed the questionable transactions made by the cardholder before certifying the billing statement for payment to the bank servicing the purchase card. Since he knew or should have known that he was certifying an improper payment when he certified the purchase card payment, the certifying officer was denied relief. *Id.*

Also, a certifying officer who certifies a voucher for payment in the full amount claimed, disregarding the fact that the accompanying records indicate an outstanding indebtedness to the government against which the sum claimed is available for offset, is accountable for any resulting overpayment. 28 Comp. Gen. 425 (1949). *See also* B-303920, Mar. 21, 2006 (facts and circumstances should have alerted certifying officer to the fact that he was improperly certifying payments to purchase bottled water for employees, an unauthorized expenditure). Similarly, certifying a voucher in the full amount within a prompt payment discount period without taking the discount will result in liability for the amount of the lost discount. However, a certifying officer is not liable for failing, even if negligently, to certify a voucher within the time discount period. 45 Comp. Gen. 447 (1966).

E. Other Relief Statutes

1. Statutes Requiring Affirmative Action

Page 9-129 – Replace the last paragraph with the following:

Since 31 U.S.C. § 3728, the primary certifying officer relief statute, does not apply to the legislative or judicial branches, Congress has enacted specific statutes for several legislative branch agencies and for the judicial branch authorizing or requiring the designation of certifying officers, establishing their accountability, and, in some cases, authorizing the Comptroller General to grant relief. Patterned after 31 U.S.C. § 3728, they are: 2 U.S.C.§ 142b (Library of Congress), 2 U.S.C. § 142e (Congressional Budget Office), 2 U.S.C. § 142*l* (Office of Compliance), 2 U.S.C. § 1904 (Capitol Police), and 44 U.S.C. § 308 (Government Printing Office). The Secretary of the Senate and the Speaker of the House of Representatives have the authority to waive the collection of erroneous payments of salary or allowances for employees of the Senate and the House, respectively. 2 U.S.C. §§ 130c, 130d. The relevant provision for the judicial branch is 28 U.S.C. § 613. *See* B-303920, Mar. 21, 2006.

Chapter 10

FEDERAL ASSISTANCE: GRANTS AND COOPERATIVE AGREEMENTS

A. INTRODUCTION

Page 10-5 – Replace footnote number 6 with the following:

[6] The *Catalog of Federal Domestic Assistance* is published by the General Services Administration and the Office of Management and Budget (OMB) pursuant to 31 U.S.C. § 6104 and OMB Circular No. A-89, *Federal Domestic Assistance Program Information* (Aug. 17, 1984). The *Catalog* is a governmentwide list of financial and nonfinancial federal assistance programs, projects, services, and activities administered by federal agencies that provide assistance or benefits to the American public. 31 C.F.R. § 205.2. The most recently updated print edition and the frequently updated online version can both be accessed through the *Catalog's* Web site at www.cfda.gov (last visited Feb. 8, 2008). In addition, OMB, on December 13, 2007, rolled out a new publicly accessible Web site that provides information on all major federal grants, loans, and contracts. *See* www.USASpending.gov (last visited Feb. 8, 2008). This Web site is in response to 2006 legislation to improve the accessibility of federal spending data, Federal Funding Accountability and Transparency Act of 2006, Pub. L. No. 109-282, 120 Stat. 1186 (Sept. 26, 2006), 31 U.S.C. § 6101 note.

B. Grants *Versus* Procurement Contracts

2. The Federal Grant and Cooperative Agreement Act

Page 10-16 – Insert the following after the first full paragraph:

An example of a statutory scheme for oversight of a grant program can be found in the Help America Vote Act of 2002 (HAVA), which authorizes various federal agencies to make grants or provide payments of federal funds to the states and various other entities for purposes related to election reform. Pub. L. No. 107-252, 116 Stat. 1666 (Oct. 29, 2002). Section 902 of HAVA authorizes each agency making a grant or payment to audit any recipient of the funds, and also provides that if the Comptroller General makes a determination as a result of an audit that a fund recipient did not comply with program requirements or received an excess payment, the recipient must return a certain portion of the payment. In B-306475, Jan. 30, 2006, GAO concluded that the provision regarding GAO audits does not supersede the independent statutory authority of agencies to audit and take corrective action on the use of federal funds, so GAO need not make its section 902 determination before a paying agency may audit and take corrective action on questioned costs. If the Comptroller General were to make a determination under HAVA as a result of any audit he conducts, he will make an appropriate recommendation for the agency to determine liability and take corrective action. *Id.*

C. Some Basic Concepts

2. Availability of Appropriations

Page 10-43 – Replace the first full paragraph with the following:

Appropriations for grant programs are generally subject to the same time availability rules as other appropriations. Adherence to the existing framework for grantmaking, as laid out in the statute and implementing regulations, provides structure and consistency, which in turn promotes the goals of proper administration and accounting, as well as fairness to all grant applicants. For example, in one case, despite apparent statutory and regulatory limitations on grants to certain colleges and graduate institutions, the Education Department had granted 4-year "extensions" to the original 5-year grants awarded to those institutions. GAO concluded that Education should strictly adhere to the statutory and regulatory duration restrictions for grant periods and terminate grants improperly extended. If, at that time, Education determined that additional assistance was warranted, the department could award a new grant to that institution or, in the alternative, seek legislative changes that would allow for extensions to 5-year grants. B-303845, Jan. 3, 2006.

Also, when Congress expressly provides that a grant appropriation "shall remain available until expended" (no-year appropriation), the funds remain available until they are obligated and expended by the grantor agency subject to the account closing statute, 31 U.S.C. § 1555. It should be emphasized that the time availability of grant appropriations governs the grantor agency's obligation and expenditure of the funds; it does not limit the time in which the grantee must use the funds once it has received them. B-289801, Dec. 30, 2002. Of course, the grant statute or the grantor agency may impose time limits on a grantee's use of funds. *See City of New York v. Shalala,* 34 F.3d 1161 (2nd Cir. 1994); *Mayor and City Council of Baltimore v. Browner,* 866 F. Supp. 249 (D. Md. 1994).

INDEX

T

U

V

W

Y

Z